HORIZONS OF ENCHANTMENT

RE-MAPPING THE TRANSNATIONAL

A Dartmouth Series in American Studies

SERIES EDITOR

Donald E. Pease

Avalon Foundation Chair of Humanities

Founding Director of the Futures of American Studies Institute

Dartmouth College

The emergence of Transnational American Studies in the wake of the Cold War marks the most significant reconfiguration of American Studies since its inception. The shock waves generated by a newly globalized world order demanded an understanding of America's embeddedness within global and local processes rather than scholarly reaffirmations of its splendid isolation. The series Re-Mapping the Transnational seeks to foster the cross-national dialogues needed to sustain the vitality of this emergent field. To advance a truly comparativist understanding of this scholarly endeavor, Dartmouth College Press welcomes monographs from scholars both inside and outside the United States.

For a complete list of books available in this series, see www.upne.com.

Lene M. Johannessen, *Horizons of Enchantment: Essays in the American Imaginary*

John Carlos Rowe, *Afterlives of Modernism: Liberalism, Transnationalism, and Political Critique*

Anthony Bogues, *Empire of Liberty: Power, Desire, and Freedom*

Bernd Herzogenrath, *An American Body|Politic: A Deleuzian Approach*

Johannes Voelz, *Transcendental Resistance: The New Americanists and Emerson's Challenge*

LENE M. JOHANNESSEN

HORIZONS OF ENCHANTMENT

Essays in the American Imaginary

DARTMOUTH COLLEGE PRESS
HANOVER, NEW HAMPSHIRE

Dartmouth College Press
An imprint of University Press of New England
www.upne.com

Manufactured in the United States of America
Designed by Katherine B. Kimball
Typeset in Sabon by Integrated Publishing Solutions,
Grand Rapids, Michigan.

Library of Congress Cataloging-in-Publication Data
appear on the last printed page of this book.

5 4 3 2 1

CONTENTS

FOREWORD

THE APTLY TERMED "transnational turn" has resulted in the most significant reconfiguration of American Studies since its inception. Transnational American Studies grew out of the conceptual transformation generated by a newly globalized world order and therefore demands an understanding of America's embeddedness within global *and* local processes rather than scholarly re-affirmations of its splendid isolation.

This emergent field has inspired projects that ascribe different significance and valuation to the word "transnational." As it shifted in its significance from the representation of an exceptional national identity to the conceptualization of multinational and trans-local interactive processes, the transnational acquired a broad range of multiple and at times contradictory meanings. For some scholars transnational constituted an accurate representation of the United States' unusual demographic and geopolitical identity. For others it invoked the transnational as a concept with which to undermine the area studies model that presupposed the isomorphism of the object of study with the continental United States. These scholars dis-associated their research from the imperial agency of "America," resituating Americanist research practices and objects of study within cross-national and transcultural circuits of production, translation, consumption and transformation.

Many of the most important works on Transnational American Studies do not presuppose the model of America Studies that developed in the United States. Scholars working outside the United States have situated Americanist research practices and objects of study within cross-national and trans-cultural circuits of production, translation, consumption and transformation. But Americanist scholars within the United States have not had access to many of the works on Transnational American Studies published outside the United States.

Dartmouth College Press's new series, Re-Mapping the Transnational, grew out of the desire to ameliorate this situation by fostering the cross-national dialogues needed to sustain the vitality of this emergent field. Re-Mapping the Transnational was founded on the premise that non-U.S. Americanists (for example, German, Swedish, Asian, Afro-Caribbean scholars) use models for thinking and writing about American Studies that are different from those deployed by United States scholars. The importance to Transnational American Studies of Lene Johannessen's monograph *Horizons of Enchantment: Essays in the American Imaginary* is evident in the cross-disciplinary dialogue it generated in its U.S. Americanist readers.

Some readers may fault Johannessen for failing to follow the lines of argument laid down by scholars of American literature based in the United States. They may specifically criticize her for using Cornelius Castoriadis's conceptualization of the Cultural Imaginary rather than, as have most United States Americanist scholars, Benedict Anderson's or Jacques Lacan's formulations.

The potential criticisms may in fact locate the fault-line distinguishing the viewpoint of U.S. based American Studies scholar from that of a "non-American" americanist. In criticizing Johannessen for introducing unconventional pairings of authors, and refusing to base her understanding of the American Imaginary on the now canonical opposition to American exceptionalism, we demonstrate how U.S. American Studies scholars can exercise the prerogatives of what might be described as disciplinary exceptionalism. When we shift the terms of our response from a description of what Johannessen has done to articulate prescriptions concerning what transnational americanist scholars should instead do, we tacitly presuppose that the relations of knowledge production that are now prevalent in U.S. academic institutions could (and should) be universalized as the normative scholarly attitude of americanist scholars worldwide.

American readers may question use of Benedict Anderson's (or Lacan's) definition of the "national imaginary" (rather than that of Castoriadis or Charles Taylor). This instruction amounts to the demand that Johannessen submit her framework of analysis to U.S. Americanists' scholarly protocols. But in Europe, Castoriadis's theorization of cultural imaginaries is considered superior to that of either Benedict Anderson or Jacques Lacan. Indeed scholars throughout Western Europe in particular consider Castoriadis foundational to the understanding of the U.S. imaginary upon which Benedict Anderson depends for his accounts of Imagined Communities.

Like other American Studies scholars working outside the United States, Lene Johannessen brings a set of academic protocols to her understanding of U.S. culture that differs from those of many United States Americanists. If these different interpretive frameworks were made to conform to existing disciplinary orthodoxies within U.S. American Studies, the entire purpose of the series would be subverted. The commentary that *Horizons of Enchantment: Essays in the American Imaginary* has already solicited from its readers discloses the critical difference that transnational scholarship perspectives can affect in the field of American Studies. I look forward to participating in this important cross-cultural conversation.

Donald Pease

PREFACE AND ACKNOWLEDGMENTS

THE CHAPTERS IN THIS BOOK may be considered field trips in the varied and conglomerated area that is American literature, or, if you like, excursions in literary and cultural archaeology. Each one has something to say about its particular subject as it is constituted by and constitutive of its own moment of origination as well as the moments it dialogues with, be it a Norwegian-American novel, its relation to the *Bildung* genre, and its ties to culturological formation; the multiple routes that constitute Rodolfo Gonzales's "I am Joaquín" into being and its relation to Walt Whitman's "Song of Myself"; Richard Ford's narrative figuration of dejected apathy against the suburban fruition of the American imaginary's ideals; or the "conversation" between the nonliterary, ideological works of Samuel Huntington and Richard Rodriguez.

Given the generic and aesthetic variation among these works, the chapters necessarily retain a certain independence from each other in terms of the approaches and theories they draw on. On the one hand, they offer new readings of both well-known and lesser-known works, sometimes in unlikely company. On the other hand, these readings do not veer from the objective hinted at in the book's title, of reading the works as refractions of and responses to the enchantment of the American imaginary. They explore, gauge, and bring out the works' varied articulations of their places in the imaginary, as well as their relations to its magic. They all engage with the American imaginary in its flexibility and continued capacity to speak to and of our fundamental human desire to give aspiration free reign, to pursue this desire within an instituted imaginary that not only encourages what Rodriguez calls the quest for "I" but also celebrates it as a socially beneficial endeavor. The conglomerated social fabric that constitutes American culture contains many reactions and reflections of the encounter with the imaginary, and consequently each chapter yields different enactments of these negotiations. This is how it must be; the accommodation extended by the imaginary as an enabling filter is filtered back into it in a dynamic and multifarious reciprocity. There is nothing earth-shattering in this, but I hope that reading according to Charles Taylor and Cornelius Castoriadis's concept of the imaginary offers a way to make sense of the glue that, to many an observer, miraculously holds America together, and provides a tool for probing the country's challenges and direction.

For our own work, we invariably rely on the support and work of friends and colleagues, near and far. The list here is far from complete, but I am grateful to the department of Foreign Languages at the University of Bergen, Norway, and to its Faculty of Humanities, for allowing me the time away from teaching and administrative chores to complete this book, and for providing me the necessary financial support to spend a semester engaged in research in the United States. I am equally indebted to the Literature Department and to Karen Bassi, department chair, at the University of California, Santa Cruz, for hosting me as a visiting researcher and for generously facilitating my stay. I am particularly grateful to Norma Klahn at UCSC for her kind support and helpful advice during our conversations; I have gained a lot of inspiration from her knowledgeable insights into the workings of cultural imaginaries. I would also like to thank Donald Pease, whose engagement with American Studies outside the United States is a source of continuing encouragement and support to many of us. My students have in various contexts brought their curiosity and unexpected perspectives to bear on some of the themes of this book, and I greatly appreciate that. Grateful acknowledgment is also made to David Chu for brilliant editorial suggestions. As always, my most heartfelt gratitude goes to all my children, who in their various ways have kindly and bravely made it possible for me to finish this book, and to Kevin, for loving support and willingness to listen.

Midway through the work on this book I received the news of Emory Elliott's sudden passing. Scholars and students across the world lost a dear friend and a highly esteemed colleague; few individuals are able to make such a difference in and touch so many lives as Professor Elliott did, and he is greatly missed. I am forever thankful for the intellectual and friendly generosity he showed me during the years I had the fortune of knowing him.

This book is dedicated to Emory.

A shorter version of the first part of chapter 5 appeared in Lene Johannessen, "The Lonely Figure: Memory of Exile in Ana Menéndez' 'In Cuba I Was a German Shepherd.'" *Journal of Postcolonial Writing* 41, no. 1 (2005): 54–68. Available from: http://www.informaworld.com. Grateful acknowledgment is made for permission to reprint this material.

A portion of chapter 6 appeared in Lene Johannessen, "Remembering America," in *Postcolonial Dislocations: Travel, History, and the Ironies of Narrative*, ed. Charles I. Armstrong and Øyunn Hestetun (Oslo: Novus Press, 2006), 123–34.

HORIZONS OF ENCHANTMENT

INTRODUCTION

A FEW YEARS AGO I was on a yearlong sabbatical in California. When it was time to pack up and return to Norway we had a yard sale, a wonderful institution possible only through a combination of pleasant temperatures and plenty of space. An elderly couple strolled by, and the man came up, not to buy anything but to ask where I was going. I told him I was just going back to Norway, but I think he heard only "Norway." He gave me a quite serious look and said matter-of-factly: "Well, you have to go where your advancement is," adding that for his own advancement, he had spent several years in Alaska. To a Norwegian, presumably not all that culturally different from an American, the words spoken and the understanding of one's purpose in life sounded inherently alien. It is not that Norwegians do not try to get ahead or that we do not feel the need to improve and make the most out of life, but I don't think that deep down we feel that these are things we must do, that they are our foremost tasks. The man spoke to me from the other side of a cultural divide, and he spoke of a very particular prescription.

Not long before this I had been coediting a collection of essays on a new edition of the Norwegian writer Drude Krog Janson's *En Saloonkeeper's Datter*, originally published in Minneapolis in 1887. For various reasons Janson spent only eleven years in the United States; the novel itself has few references to America as such and for the most part takes place either in Norway or within the Norwegian community in Minnesota, the cultural parameters in both cases being largely the same. Furthermore, the novel was written in

Norwegian for a Norwegian-reading and Norwegian-speaking audience. And yet, the novel, translated in 2002 as *A Saloonkeeper's Daughter*, was by and large and without hesitation considered an American novel. I fully agree that it is indeed an American text, but the question has stuck: what makes it so?

On a personal as well as professional level, the two incidents that I have discussed served as catalysts subtly to challenge and test the understanding I thought I had of "America." By extension, questions concerning the meaning of cultural provenance and purpose crystallized for me. They made clear that, for all the similarities between (in this case) northwestern European and American cultures, and for all the overlapping that necessarily occurs in histories of immigration and in the emergent cultural rims that connect multiple spaces, certain delicate differences defy the clear explanations we would like to create. I am not really asking with J. Hector St. John de Crèvecoeur, what is an American? Nor am I asking, what is American literature? Rather, I am interested in pursuing the vague contours of the definite certainties of identification that arise from the two quandaries that I have related. How may this contradiction, this paradox, of formless and indistinct firmness and assurance, be examined and calibrated in cultural forms? This question runs through the following chapters. The field of exploration is mainly literature, ranging from the somewhat obscure Drude Krog Janson to Walt Whitman to Ana Menéndez and Richard Ford, among others; but the study also draws on other sources: essayist Richard Rodriguez and political scientist Samuel Huntington, the cultural architectonics of a Norwegian region, and the film *Sugar*. Taken together, the readings cover generic, historical, and cultural grounds that may seem to have little in common, yet despite the discrepancies and unlikeliness of dialogue, these literary and cultural texts are all, at one level or another, engaged in and with the American social imaginary, propagating, repudiating, adapting, revising, and questioning its sway and its premises.

The value of the concept of the imaginary as a methodological lens resides partly in its conceptual echo of the paradoxical nature of "vague certainty" of identification, as a simultaneously enabling and enabled cultural filter. I apply the concept as it has been elaborated in the writings of the philosophers Charles Taylor and Cornelius Castoriadis, whose expositions of the concept, its implications, and its redactions may meaningfully be brought to bear on the specifically American social imaginary. This imaginary dwells in certain archaic structures of feelings, in the sense that its framing sway hails from a conception of order above and beyond nation and culture per se and obtains instead through a sacred-secular system in which the obligation to perform and succeed individually is also a social duty. At this point the American imaginary departs most radically from its Western cousins, in its reliance on a kind of modern magic, which may be characterized loosely as a fundamental and unwavering faith in the secular sanctity of what we have come to think of as the American project of modernity.

In their significance as a resilient axis of culturological continuity, the above elements have been taken up in varied scholarly contexts by scholars such as Robert Bellah and Sacvan Bercovitch, to mention only two. Bellah's influential essay "Civil Religion in America" is a strong argument for the existence of an institutionalized religious ideology parallel to specific denominations. (The United States does not have a state religion.) He suggests that, "What we have, then, from the earliest years of the republic is a collection of beliefs, symbols, and rituals with respect to sacred things and institutionalized in a collectivity. This religion—there seems no other word for it—while not antithetical to and indeed sharing much in common with Christianity, was neither sectarian nor in any specific way Christian."[1] By reading presidential inaugural addresses and drawing on such documents as Benjamin Franklin's *Autobiography*, Bellah shows the remarkable and paradoxical existence of a religious, public framework that is able to accommodate the specificities of private, denominational manifestations. I return to the malleability that this eccentric relationship enables in connection with what I call the magic of the American imaginary. Of course, the spirituality of America as project in the world has, in other contexts, been authoritatively delineated in Bercovitch's seminal writings. Here, however, I am most interested in his explorations of cultural identification in terms of the metaphor of the chess game variation. Its potency is that of "a move which opens up a new set of possibilities within standard rules and regulations of play. . . . It's brilliant insofar as the variation leads us to a deeper understanding of how the rules work."[2] Bercovitch's chess analogy will be referred to several times further, but for now I point out the resonance of the flexibility of Bellah's notion of civil religion with the similar emphasis of Bercovitch on new sets of possibilities in the chess variation metaphor.

The readings in this book bring out different enactments of the variation and invite different views of how the rules of the game, at once malleable and constant, apply and do not apply. Given the disparate nature of the texts and the cultural forms that constitute the field of exploration, the methodological approaches are also necessarily different. None, however, veers very far from the overarching questions and framework briefly alluded to earlier: What are the limitations and possibilities of the imaginary and its variation(s)? How do we read (for) the magic of vague certainty? The implications and extractions of the imaginary, as the concept figures in Taylor and Castoriadis's work, may also be helpful when thinking about sameness and difference within a cultural and social space that we assume to share and understand. For instance, as the following chapters' readings show, certain calibrations can be made in relation to the unyielding culturological continuities specific to the American imaginary.[3] More to the point, texts' refractions of that imaginary also shed light on its contours and potentiality as it continuously adapts and evolves as an umbrella under which other kinds of imaginaries can be subsumed. This has consequences for how we think about our own Western modernity, all too often collapsed into one single perspective. And as the world has in some ways become smaller and the processes of globalization have continued, often in the guise of Americanization, the uniformity of Western cultures has been assumed, in contradistinction to cultures elsewhere: so-called traditional, religious, and tribal cultures, circumscribed by communal values contained in longstanding practices of mediation, and in various degrees serving as buffers against the encroachments of modernity. In relation to such displays of multiple or alternative modernities, it may be equally compelling to think about the fissures and elements of discord that thrive within our own, presumably identical, space, as a kind of miniature laboratory for studying the constitution of variants of modernity.

I pause here to add that I do not wish to enter into a discussion of American exceptionalism and its nature, genesis, and future. But the term does cast a long shadow on the kind of discourse I am engaging in, and a brief comment is appropriate. As countless studies over the years have shown, exceptionalism as ideological and cultural emblem has orchestrated the beginnings and continuations of the New World in fundamental ways. Thus, Deborah Madsen, one of the many who have participated in this line of inquiry, introduces her study with the statement that "American exceptionalism permeates every period of American history and is the single most powerful agent in a series of arguments that have been fought down the centuries concerning the identity of America and Americans."[4] Yet the near-paralyzing effect that the word "exceptionalism" tends to have on conversations should be addressed. Does the command of the concept itself signal, like one of its most potent expressions, Manifest Destiny, a position that is somehow beyond query, or, perhaps like "America" itself, does it forever elude exact identification and hence function as a kind of analytical deterrent? Against such mystification, one could, as Winfried Fluck does in a rather sober manner, simply accept the concept as just that, a concept: While the very term "exceptionalism" designated the "ideology of a promised land and a chosen people," he says, abandoning the ideology it stands for does not mean that we also have "to give up the idea that the development of American culture has taken place under conditions of its own." These conditions are moreover characteristic of more general movements pertaining to modernity, but they are not constellated in the same way in all countries.[5]

Fluck's admonition is extremely valid, and in some ways indispensable. Recognizing difference does not necessarily imply advocacy of imperialist agendas, support for abiding values of individualism, or claims to uniqueness, although imperialist agendas and abiding values of individualism and uniqueness are certainly also part of American history and hence make their way into the grammar of analysis. It is perfectly legitimate to approach and study American literary and cultural legacies and prospects without making claims to universalizing authority; indeed, it would be a rather odd situation were it not. Djelal Kadir says as much when he observes that "American culture has labored mightily since the inception of its history to differentiate itself as unique and exceptional. In so doing, it conforms to every other national culture in history."[6] A healthy skepticism toward the thwarting effect of discourses centered on the exceptional nature of American exceptionalism is consequently in order, not least because, as Fluck goes on to argue, "If we give up the goal of understanding these different conditions [that are non-axiologically peculiar to the United States], then we will be helpless in the face of a United States that, currently more than ever, is indeed dealing with other nations on conditions of its own."[7] Fluck's observations are made in the context of the drive during recent decades toward the internationalization and transnationalization of American Studies, but his comment goes beyond the concerns of institutionalized study only. As several of the readings that follow will explore, the transnational and transcultural have been ingrained in American culture from day one, but the crossings and movements between and beyond disparate social imaginaries should not be understood as in any way taking place on equal terms. Indeed, the potency of the American imaginary even now commands participation in its magic on its own terms. That may be almost unique in the world, although I do not believe it really is: every imaginary instructs subjection to its instituting grids in order to prevail. And as Richard Rodriguez observes via a quotation from Marshall McLuhan, "the moment America's culture becomes the culture of the world it is no longer American culture."[8]

The question that crystallized from the incidents I related initially, of having to go where one's advancement is, and of wondering why a Norwegian novel is in fact an American one, concerns what we assume about the term "America" as much as it concerns what, how, or indeed, as Arif Dirlik has asked, when the adjective "American" may signify.[9] The ambiguity configured through the components that constitute the variation, "vague" and "certainty," allows for any number of interpellations and interpretations, and yet the responses in play seem oddly and unyieldingly continuous, in relation not only to individual textual articulations but also to how these are received and commented on. Thus, chapter 1 opens with a consideration of Anna Boden and Ryan Fleck's film *Sugar*, which relates a classic story about a Dominican baseball player hoping to make it big. Now, described like that, *Sugar* sounds like just another dime-a-dozen movie about the American dream, but this is far from the case. With great depth and perception the film illustrates some of the nuances and strains underlying the magic of the American imaginary as it plays out in the proverbial field of dreams.

Preliminary reflections relating to *Sugar* lead to a more detailed discussion of the imaginary and some of its conceptual and methodological significations as these are explicated by Taylor and Castoriadis. As I have already suggested, the merit of their argument regarding the question of the imaginary is its disengagement from traditions imbued with conditions and projections of concomitant, generic expectations that stem from the kind of embedded ideological stances coming out of the same predicament as the magic itself. It is my hope that, by employing a different vocabulary to an area that trails the aforementioned and sometimes diffuse shadows of exceptionalism, two things are achieved: First, we may approach the object of study as demystified, as inherently singular in the universal sense that Kadir's statement quoted earlier suggests. Second, we gain potentially renewed and renewing insight into that same object.

The field proper for reading for the magic of the American imaginary begins with the novel that I have already mentioned, *A Saloonkeeper's Daughter*. Upon its republication in 2002, the novel was immediately welcomed as an important contribution to American literature, and classified accordingly. Orm Øverland, who has extensively annotated and introduced the new edition, observes that "For an important period of her life, [Drude Krog Janson] was an American writer. She can now be considered, in translation, for the distinctive qualities of her contribution to American literature."[10] Chapter 2 of the present volume, "'Perpetual Progress' in Drude Krog Janson's *A Saloonkeeper's Daughter*," examines this novel as a marvelously narrated turn of spirit aspiring to an individual's reinvention. The idea of a shining potential and future shows the protagonist turning her back on the old world, which shifts the tropological references to a quickening embrace of new paths, of futures rid of the imaginaries of the past. The novel can be read as an archetypal illustration of the seamless convergence between individual and society at a very specific time in American history, when the tenor of the resulting conversation echoes the ideological principles of the classical bildungsroman. Astrid Holm's example stands for a near-perfect confluence between the promise and its realization; her turn accurately reflects ideal *Bildung*: "Bildung comes from Bild (image) and so means the process of imposing an image or form on something, or the results of such a process."[11] In this it of course replicates countless other immigrant stories as conversion narratives—*Bildung* as formation from within and from without, and the imaginary as enabled and enabling filter. For we must bear in mind, as Jeffrey Sammons puts it, that a "question such as the definition of the Bildungsroman is an issue not confined to academic discourse, but [is one that] spreads into the ideological self-understanding of the culture as a whole."[12] *A Saloonkeeper's Daughter* is in fact an American novel, but the attribution has to do with the mode of conversation that it taps into and connects with, a discourse organized according to a tropological landscape, which was and is unmistakably American in constitution and perpetuation. Consequently, the tropology of the American master imaginary may be tentatively registered in this chapter, but it is only against a much broader backdrop that it can be meaningfully measured.

Chapter 3, "Songs of Different Selves: Whitman and Gonzales," examines the epic "Song of Myself" (1887 [1855]) against and alongside Gonzales's equally epic but lesser-known "I am Joaquín" (1967). Of greatest importance here is how these two foundational texts elucidate the tension between different interpretations of the imaginary. Whitman sings a self into the fabric without rifts, without seams. His are a horizontal outlook and a narrative orientation accommodating difference into the great fold and thus sounding marching orders for a national cultural narrative that is uniquely capable of transference. This all-embracing inclusiveness is both constitutive of and constituted by the American social imaginary at a very early historical-cultural stage, but it is inherently imagined. If the social imaginary can generally be described, in Taylor's words, as "the ways in which people imagine their social existence, how they fit together with others, how things go on between them and their fellows, the expectations that are normally met, and the deeper normative notions and images that underlie these expectations," then Whitman paradoxically runs up against the very constraints that the American imaginary sets up.[13] Normative notions and images in this case rest on a tropics of difference, firmly rooted in an Anglo-Saxon religious and contractual view of individual and society that does not and cannot allow for the metaphorical transference Whitman lays out. His position as ur-American poet thus seems to rest on a cultural aesthetics of mere promise, a phantasmagoria of limitless opportunity.

Such a stance signifies very differently from Rodolfo "Corky" Gonzales's poem, which delineates and excavates five centuries of forgotten legacies along a line that stays grounded in an imaginary originating within the United States: the Mexican borderland, itself reflecting the aftershocks of a fissure between differently emerging modern imaginaries competing for spatial institutions. Gonzales's "I cry and sing the same" rehearses Whitman's "I celebrate myself" but reroutes Whitman's unbridled optimism and all-embracing, future-oriented energy toward a response that gazes backward and points toward the future with both reproach and defiance. The dialogue sets up "cry" against "celebrate," and the singing of self as metaphor of nation is countered with a conflicted self who is constituted into being differently, into a social imaginary whose potential influence has returned in our own time with renewed force. There are various possible extrapolations from this, but we can tentatively suggest that Whitman's image, for all his idealization of the imaginary as a lasting articulation of the mythological anchoring of society, remains with us to this day.

One manifestation of this is the promise of the suburb, a gestalt that may be conceived according to Castoriadis's category of specific "second-order institutions," as "the essential embodiments of what is of vital importance to that societal institution."[14] From its beginnings in the 1920s (and indeed even before that), the ideological particularities of this living and lived space were precisely those of reflection: "Always as much an idea as a reality, the landscape of American suburbia has become and remained something of a symbolic minefield, the mirror (or, perhaps better put, the picture window) through which middle-class American culture casts its uneasy reflective gaze on itself."[15] And some of the most disturbing and profound reactions to the imaginary may hail precisely from this landscape of picture windows. Chapter 4 therefore focuses on an expression we often ignore as constituting this kind of reaction, even as a negation of the premises and promises of the imaginary. Numerous literary voices have sounded its notes: Crane, Fitzgerald, Faulkner, John Barth, Walker Percy, and John Cheever are just a few representatives of this strain. They have created a pantheon of souls whose predicament may perhaps be summarized in another "lost soul's" words: "Man exists only in so far as he is separated from his surroundings. The cranium is a space-traveler's helmet. Stay inside or you perish."[16] With his portrayal of the apathetic subject in the fold of postmodern suburbia, Richard Ford in *The Sportswriter* gives existential crisis a contemporary form on the foremost stage of the imaginary. It is fitting that the last novel proper to figure in the present work is premised on precisely suburban finitudes: in a disheartening echo of the infinitude of Whitman's creation, aspiration and defeat are locked in an impossible embrace. The suburb's promise is, ultimately, the promise of a self-reliance that as enabling filter becomes a condition of stasis.

Chapter 5, "'Relations Stretched Out' in the American Imaginary," reads two representations of very different, diametrically opposed engagements with the imaginary. Ana Menéndez's retrospective short story collection from 2001, *In Cuba I Was a German Shepherd*, offers various narratives from the Cuban exile community in Miami. The fact that they are informed precisely by exile allows for an exploration of a particular version of encounter in and with the American migratory. A distinctive kind of memory choreographs these stories' discourse, and its figurations and figures only marginally engage with the imaginary. Herein lie the contours of a different kind of engagement, for some reflections of the proverbial pond remain dark, unyielding. I suggest that Menéndez's work stands as an illustration of a strand in which the imagination that enters into the space of the American imaginary retreats, creates itself over again in its own image rather than that of the imaginary, and thus is extremely different from what is examined in chapter 2. This has implications for the social fabric and allegorizes the path of other imaginaries, which, in various ways, by choice or by force, have been excluded from transition into the master imaginary.

A completely opposing version of this encounter is the adaptation that so immerses itself in the imaginary that it brings the imaginary with it when it leaves. For this second part of chapter 5 I draw on the cultural history of a specific region in southern Norway, a case illustrating the transposition of elements from the American imaginary in a reversed and selective process by which what pertains at the outset to the symbolic sphere is instituted elsewhere. Similarly, this case tells us something about the capacity for transference that the American imaginary possesses and the acts of remembering and preferences in processes of cultural bridging, translation, and representation. Both Menéndez's short stories and the history of the Lister region are ultimately also commentaries on modalities of migration and cultural memory as these are mapped out in memory and scripture, be they in writing or in architecture, as spatial and temporal relations, in Doreen Massey's words, "stretch out."[17]

The last chapter of the present volume, "Recalling America," also hinges on memory and further explores the tension between different conceptions of the imaginary, its originations, and future. In *Who Are We? The Challenges to America's National Identity* (2004), the late Samuel Huntington launched what may be read as a regrounding of the American social imaginary according to an East-West orientation, thereby detracting from the allure of the all-embracing mirage that Whitman so convincingly schematized. The "conversation" that this chapter stages between Huntington's *Who Are We?* and Richard Rodriguez's *Brown: The Last Discovery of America* thus turns on culturological self-understandings that have been part of the discourse of America about itself from the beginning. From an outside position both are correct: Huntington's gauging of what American culture is, is not incorrect; but neither is Rodriguez's, which concerns the unrelenting process of literal and figurative "browning." The latter's position also has its echoes in aesthetics; the manifesto of Guillermo Gómez-Peña and his ensemble *Pocho Nostra*, for instance, states:

> As ghost citizens of a borderless nation, we may soon have to redefine the meanings of a long list of dated 20th-century terminology. Words such as "immigrant," "alien," "foreigner," "minority," "diaspora," "border," and "American" may no longer be useful to explain our new condition, identity and dilemmas.[18]

In the light of observations such as these, the question arises, Do the multiple social imaginaries that reflect on the master imaginary, in tandem with significant changes in the ethnic and cultural fabric, approximate a version of Huntington's original, or do they splinter into multiple ossifications? Or is the malleability of the American imaginary such that it is endlessly accommodating? Doubts lie beneath the surface, not only throughout this book but also in broader discourses of political and social impact. And if it be the case that all the doubts and fears and hopes in the end center on the vague question of values, then one must also ask, according to whose standards, whose imaginary?

[1]

THE IMAGINARY

A Cold and Broken Hallelujah

To introduce the more strictly methodological concerns of this chapter, I want to briefly consider Ryan Fleck and Anna Boden's baseball film *Sugar* (2008).[1] Its engagement with the religious metaphoricity of the game itself, ambivalence of purpose, frustration, and, ultimately, questions of interpreting the signs of magic, may serve as an appropriate lead-in to the broader issues at stake. *Sugar* traces the fictional story of a young Dominican pitcher's entry into the American major leagues; the film immediately found its place in the hall of fame of baseball movies. However, unlike classics such as *Eight Men Out* (1988), *Bull Durham* (1988), *Field of Dreams* (1989), *The Natural* (1994), *The Rookie* (2002), and *The Sandlot* (1993), to mention several, *Sugar* is not really about the game itself, and it certainly does not proffer the classical, home-run ending. Instead it ends on a rather hesitant note that comments with profound insight on the limitless possibilities held out by the prospect of playing in the major leagues, which is, of course, a trope firmly lodged within the larger one of advancement and aspiration.

The story is familiar: dreaming of fame and glory at Yankee Stadium in New York, Miguel "Sugar" Santos lives and breathes baseball. The epitome of his dream is to buy a Cadillac that runs on water, an absurd contrast to the impoverished streets he hails from. The film opens with Santos's practicing pitching in one of the major leagues' many "academies," or "factories," where, as Andrew O'Hehir puts it, the Dominican Republic's "raw talent is nurtured for North American harvest in a sort of plantation system controlled by Major League Baseball teams, in the movie the fictitious Kansas City Knights."[2] And Santos makes it. A scout drafts him for a minor-league spring training camp in Arizona, and from there he goes on to a small town in Iowa to play for a Single-A, minor-league club. The process is matter-of-factly narrated: there are no melodramatic scenes of outright exploitation or abuse. If anything, the viewer is offered a rare glimpse into the detached workings of the system of big-league business. The directors know the game, and so do the protagonists. The game is about winning or losing: baseball can never end in a tie, and it is all about numbers. As one character tells Santos, "Life gives you many chances; baseball gives you only one." Santos harbors no illusions of easy success. He knows the odds, and early on, while he is still in the Dominican Republic, a friend lets on that he, too, once dreamed of the major leagues. He went and returned. The exchange, whereupon Santos confidently proclaims that, unlike his friend, he will succeed, lends a lingering ambiguity to the story's pace.

Having pitched a number of excellent games for his new team in Iowa, Santos begins throwing wild. At one point the manager yanks him and replaces him with another recently arrived Dominican sensation. In a moment Santos sees just how expendable he is, that any number of guys just like him are ready to take the mound, and that managers will not hesitate to bring in fresh arms and new blood. He decides to quit the team before the team quits him, and he goes to New York to join a former teammate who was sent packing after getting hurt in a game. The last part of the movie takes place in the Bronx, in one of New York's Dominican neighborhoods. It ends there, with Santos pitching again, on a playing field at Roberto Clemente State Park.

The depiction of Miguel Santos may be fictional, but that fiction has thousands of counterparts in real life, as the public's reception of Boden and Fleck demonstrated when the movie was first screened in Santo Domingo: "they got it right." What they got right, among other things, are the rather deplorable facts pertaining to how, as O'Hehir puts it, "a beloved American game has become a peculiar quasi-colonial enterprise."[3] Much could be said about this enterprise and the economic, political, and cultural system it both feeds and feeds off of. A comment made by Cuban baseball historian Roberto González Echevarría illuminates some of the stakes involved:

> I take a dim view of what the major leagues are doing in the Dominican Republic with these so-called baseball academies, where children are being signed at a very early age and not being cared for. Most of them are providing the context for the stars to emerge; if you take 100 baseball players in those academies, or 100 baseball players anywhere, only one of them will play even an inning in the major leagues. The others are there as a supporting cast.[4]

Sugar illustrates Echevarría's pessimism with objective accuracy and without judgment, but certain inferences are hard not to draw. The dialogue following the injury of Santos's friend and his subsequent dismissal from the team, for instance, has disturbing undertones. Santos wonders aloud how they can be treated as animals. If one bears in mind that the name for the roster of relief pitchers, as well as the actual area where they sit and warm up during a game, is the "bull pen," Santos's comment assumes a darkly dehumanizing tenor. The growing realization of how easily Santos and his countrymen can be discarded and the dire consequences of failure are contrasted with the situation of another teammate, drafted from Stanford University. If he fails in the minor leagues, he can go back to studying history; if Santos fails, he must return to a poverty-stricken and jobless Dominican Republic.

The most eloquent and startling scenes in *Sugar* are those set in New York, where Santos gets a dishwashing job and begins a new life. At no point in this part of the movie do we hear English spoken, and the range of the many characters' places of origin, and their varieties of Spanish, constitute a curiously and genuinely pan-American scene. The wide shots of New York streets give the city's "original," Anglo-Saxon identity away, but letting the Latino conglomerate literally overlay that cultural character produces an effective commentary on what has become known popularly as the changing face of America. The dialogues between the protagonists reflect the diversity hidden by the visual images and bring home the multifariousness of a group commonly perceived simply as Latinos, or, in some cases, collapsed into the single category "Mexican."[5]

A Spanish version of Leonard Cohen's "Hallelujah" accompanies some of the last shots, making a compelling and deeply touching comment on the destiny of Santos and so many of the other characters. The repetition in the lyrics of "it's a cold and it's a broken Hallelujah" brings to the narrative the seriousness of undisclosed truth. The line plays with the ambiguity of a defeat that is simultaneous with a kind of victory by evoking the original promise of potential advancement and the disappointments to be maneuvered through. Moreover, the song foreshadows the full impact of the very last scene. Having found his friend, Santos is encouraged to come and play ball in the neighborhood ballpark. Several other players are there when he arrives, and they introduce themselves in a touching and powerful sequence of close-up frames, each listing his name, field position, former minor and major league teams, and country of origin. The catalogue impresses on the viewer the countless players such as Santos whom the academies have trained, tried, and thrown away, and it reminds us that, as former pitcher for the San Diego Padres Brendan Sullivan III puts it: if they avoid returning home to "the poverty they came from [they can] try to eke out an existence at menial labor in the States, with nothing left over except tales of their playing days chasing the dream."[6] The last shot of the movie shows Santos on the bench with an inscrutable look on his face. A quiet smile slowly spreads over his face, perhaps in recognition of a renewed love of the game itself, and, oddly, of the team he has now been drafted onto. It is, finally, no coincidence that the field they play on is named after the legendary Puerto Rican right fielder Roberto Clemente, the first Latino player to make it to the Hall of Fame.

Sugar is a curiously apt illustration of the American imaginary in its subtle engagement with the sacred and secular trimmings of structural embedding, all at once. Two figures stand out. One is the repetition of "Hallelujah"; the other is the structure provided by the game of baseball itself as a metaphor for the dream and promise that America continues to offer. These are well-worn phrases, but it would be foolish not to recognize the abiding authority they hold, now as much as ever. All of this may sound like a rehashing of old tropes, of the presumed universalism of things American. The argument, however, is broader than that, observing that the pace of modern processes quickens and slows, and that some tracks have struck a balance between understandings of individual and communal obligations and responsibilities in ways that attract and accommodate more easily than other tracks. What that means is that we find our places within different imaginaries differently. In *Sugar*, the baseball field and its potential become metaphors for the sacredness of the communal conviction that the game is right, even as they invite individual performance and aspiration within its rules. As the film closes with the catalogue of frustrated hopes that have been collated into a team that continues to play the game, it tactfully remarks that the game "supports a sense of uniformity, a sense of belonging to a vast, extended American formality that attends the same church."[7] The hallelujah may be cold and broken, but it is still a form of praise. The unresolved continuity of this particular variation is the same as that lodged in the vague certainty of the American imaginary, which we now approach from a more methodological angle.

Imaginary/Image

The imaginary is one of those concepts we intuitively use and know. One of its common interpretations is that of mirroring, the imaginary as an image *of* something. As a consequence, the use of the term often slips into a repertory of more or less vague significations, which is not necessarily a bad thing. But in the discussions that follow, I spend a little time on getting at its more exact contours, to the extent this is possible. I employ the imaginary in specific ways, relying mainly on Charles Taylor's *Modern Social Imaginaries* and Cornelius Castoriadis's *Imaginary Institution of Society*, as well as some of the latter's essays gathered more recently in *Figures of the Thinkable*. The excavations of the idea and manifestations of the imaginary in these two thinkers complement and diverge from each other in interesting ways, even as their overall assessments are nearly identical. I begin with Taylor's general definition of the social imaginary: "the ways in which people imagine their social existence, how they fit together with others, how things go on between them and their fellows, the expectations that are normally met, and the deeper normative notions and images that underlie these expectations."[8] Such characteristics are shared by all societies as the necessary understanding of the glue that keeps the village, the group, or the nation reasonably coherent in culture and politics, in relation to different understandings and glues. Thus far the description roughly conforms to Benedict Anderson's seminal observations on imagined communities, which Taylor also acknowledges. One reason why the concept of the imaginary tends to erode is the slippage in its usage to the specular, which is associated with the root "image" and its derivatives "imagine" and "imagination." The boundaries here are of great concern especially to Castoriadis, who stresses that "The imaginary of which I am speaking is not an image *of*. It is the unceasing and essentially *undetermined* (social-historical and psychical) creation of *figures/forms/images*, on the basis of which alone there can ever be a question of something. What we call 'reality' and 'rationality' are its works."[9]

"Creativity" here is related to what Castoriadis later refers to as radical imagination, denoting the human faculty to produce images, to create ex nihilo, a uniquely human ability that precedes and conditions everything else we are capable of:

> I call that imagination "radical" because the creation of representations, affects, and desires by the human imagination is subject to conditions, but never predetermined. . . . [It] is also at the root of another extraordinary ability of human beings; the ability to symbolize. It is thanks to the radical imagination that human beings are able to see a thing in another thing."[10]

It is important that we maintain the distinction between imagination and imaginary in these senses fairly rigidly before us; their variation does have consequences for how we proceed to understand the imaginary in relation to what Taylor calls embedding and even enchanting functions. What may be broadly characterized as a Lacanian specular interpretation of the imaginary is not of use here, even if we do not agree with Castoriadis that it is "vulgar reductionism."[11] At the same time, the implications of "imaginary" in nonspecular usage are related, and the following passage elucidates their proximity, as well as their complex relationship. It also speaks more generally to Castoriadis's stance on the concept of the imaginary:

> I talk about the imaginary because the history of humanity is the history of the human imaginary and its works (*oeuvres*). And I talk about the history and works of the radical imaginary, which appears as soon as there is any human collectivity. It is the instituting social imaginary that creates institutions in general (the institutions as form) as well as the particular institutions of each specific society, and the radical imagination of the singular human being.[12]

The distinction resides, then, in a split between the individual as carrier of radical imagination and the collective as carrier of the imaginary, but with the two simultaneously, inextricably linked in a co-constitutive, creative relationship. For the purposes of this study, which not only explores how literary texts and cultural forms imagine their spaces in relation to those of others in the context of "America" but also more concretely examines the ways they refract, uphold, and as literary realities modify and calibrate the historical society they partake in, the idea of the imaginary is useful. My aim here is not to focus on imaginaries of completely different origination, which represent alternative ways of being in the world in relation to the American imaginary. Rather, it is to pursue readings of active responses to and participation in the ongoing process of the "creation of figures/forms/images" within it. Such (literary) encounters in turn test and gauge the continuities and possible aberrations of the currents and sensibilities that constitute the American imaginary. Hence, my readings attempt to calibrate how the imaginary's contours materialize, or, in Castoriadis's terminology, are instituted. In this respect, the strategy of reading *for*, instead of reading *of*, takes a cue from the core principle underlying Mikhail Bakhtin's work, which, in relation to a culturological project, is best expressed as follows:

> The problem of any particular domain of culture taken as a whole, whether it be cognition, ethics, or art, can be understood as the prob-

> lem of this domain's boundaries. . . . every cultural act lives essentially on the boundaries, and it derives its seriousness and significance from this fact. Separated by abstraction from these boundaries, it loses the ground of its being and becomes vacuous, arrogant, it degenerates and dies.[13]

The social imaginary—the history of human collectivity and the radical imaginary—similarly cannot exist in isolation. Whichever society and institutions we talk about, they feed off of a multiplicity of encounters, remakings, and reimaginings, which they in turn feed, for the defining and renewing potential inherent in each hinges on its ability to react to, respond to, and, finally, accommodate a querying outside. Hence, attention must be paid to the always-creative potential of the encounter and the space that opens up on variously emergent boundaries.

That stated, it is obvious that the particularly American social imaginary is also a rather disorderly one, because there is not one American social imaginary, but several. Or more correctly, there is one, but it operates on a different level, as what I suggest is a master imaginary, a canvassing trope that has a seemingly unlimited capacity for engendering other, alternative imaginaries out of its fold, depending on what it mirrors. This master imaginary stretches outward as irresistible promise, and is refracted in all its vastness in the simple phrase: "You have to go where your advancement is." Not knowing what he did, the elderly man spoke a remarkable sentence that taps into the very heart of the American master imaginary's magic: obligatory self-interest combined with the idea of moving forward and ahead for the common good, a duty to be performed, embedded in the simple last words of the Declaration of Independence, "and the pursuit of happiness." The sentence, as Taylor notes, resonates with the purpose of the nation itself, but more than that, it constitutes the kernel of a modern social imaginary through which the individual, free from traditional conceptions and restraints of religious or divine law, as well as the duties of order handed down from centuries of traditions and civic laws, can pursue his or her own interpretation of roles and society. What is most compelling about such a scenario is that the perpetuation of ideas that spawn this purpose, this very particular kind of liberty and experiment, forms a set of beliefs that is strangely sacred in all its secularity (I am not referring to the strong position of religion in the United States, which is unique in an otherwise rather secular West) and may place American culture closer to other faith-based communities than its Western cousins. It accounts for the extremely flexible, yet universal and eternal, appeal of the said project, which always invites and indeed accepts new interpretations—up to a point. For the imaginary and its magic never lose sight of the anchoring in the rules of the game for which they provide the playground. In Sacvan Bercovitch's words, "America" is a "language game of malleable beginnings and possible futures," quite different from its "old world" relatives, where nationality "remains an endgame puzzle: identity to be resolved in three or four moves." This is another way of approaching the genius of what Bercovitch refers to as the variation, its magic as perpetually recommencing, or as he elegantly phrases it, newness as a "continual movement toward endings that issues in an endless affirmation of beginnings." The variation therefore continues to have a powerful capacity to raise possibilities even as anticipations and beliefs in the rules of the game abide: they must "apply situationally, hence malleably."[14] There is of course nothing particularly magical, in the sense of elusive and supernatural, about chess or baseball; there is, however, something magical about what Bercovitch calls the "American game," or what I here call the American imaginary, as a totality of combined individual and communal conviction, presents. Much of it has to do with what Taylor calls *enchantment*, but understood here in an oddly modern manner.

Imaginary and Symbolism

Let me backtrack a little. To go on about the magic of the American imaginary would return us squarely within the range of the American dream, to say the least. As I have already suggested, I do not see this as inherently useless, for on some level that dream is the lifeblood of the American imaginary. And it bears repeating that, while all societies are orchestrated according to imaginaries peculiar to their specificities, not all societies are structured on an idiosyncratically elusive concept such as a dream: to speak of the Swedish dream, the Greek dream, or the Guatemalan dream does not evoke the slightest signification. The applicability of this peculiar variation is therefore restricted, for it does not transfer in the entirety of its embedding potential to other spaces, except in cases of self-conscious attempts to adapt and emulate similar structures of feeling. Then, however, we would speak not of whole societal or cultural complexes but of isolated occurrences in which the American dream is re-presented as an image *of*. This is important, because an image *of* lacks the dynamism of reciprocity and portability that is key to the continuities of any living culture. This would echo the reductionism of the specular that Castoriadis attributes to Lacanian interpretations of the imaginary. The many images of something in this case are like snapshots in a wallet, put away and usable as reminders, but not as active participants in the life of what they reflect. From the outside, and, in reality, from within, the dream as image *of* occupies a somewhat static sphere of potentiality and reference. The fault line between it and the imaginary as yardsticks for making the comparisons and calibrations between participants runs along the institution, to which we now turn in more detail.

Castoriadis's general position and departure point on the imaginary have already been noted, but to understand his observations on the institution we need to begin with the arguments he makes regarding the symbolic. Castoriadis is adamant that "the imaginary has to use the symbolic not only to 'express' itself (this is self-evident), but to 'exist', to pass from the virtual to anything more than this."[15] The elucidation of this relationship runs along a track on which the symbolic and the imaginary are inextricably interwoven: the imaginary has to use the symbolic in order to pass into actualization, and the imaginary faculty is an absolute prerequisite for bringing symbols into being in the first place, at which point the institution of those images can follow. Castoriadis cites religion, which is universal to human cultures, as one of the more apposite examples, and the following quotation concerning Mosaic law makes clear the kinds of questions he pursues:

> It will be said that at one stage of the evolution of human societies, the institution of an imaginary possessing a greater reality than the real itself—God, or, more generally, a religious imaginary—"conforms to the ends" of society, follows from real conditions, and fills an essential function. . . . Why do we find, in every case, at the heart of this imaginary and in all of its expressions something that cannot be reduced to the functional, an original investment by society of the world and itself with meaning—meanings which are not "dictated" by real factors since it is instead this meaning that attributes to these real factors a particular importance and a particular place in the universe constituted by a given society—a meaning that can be recognized in both the content and the style of its life[?][16]

This argument posits that what essentially begins in and as the imaginary, once it gets a foothold explaining functionally the realities of a given society, immediately proceeds to institute itself, to transpose itself into the very real parameters within which people orient themselves. In the concrete case of religion, the manifestations of this process lead to churches, to certain everyday customs that must be observed, to hierarchical structures that uphold the various parts of the now instituted imaginary that its members take for granted as reality.

There is consequently a very serious aspect to these nuances, for if we conflate imagination, the dream, and the imaginary, we risk relegating particular cultural and institutional practices and understandings to a backseat, which may lead to neglect, politically as well as sociohistorically. The specular imagination and the dream are not capable of producing change or influencing the life of a society until they are instituted as imaginaries, when they immediately become pillars of real and realizable cultural constructs. In other words, if we persist in referring to imagination and the dream, we absolve the institutions of the cultural body of a society or a nation, which are after all where sociohistorical decisions are made or not made. Beneath the grids that uphold the instituted imaginary, which Castoriadis terms "second-order imaginaries," there is a central imaginary that has orchestrated into being entire such complexes of societal structures. I shall return to the more detailed aspects of

Castoriadis's elaborations throughout individual chapters. Here I note that the imaginary and the symbolic are, ultimately, never very far apart: they relate to each other as coterminously instituting and instituted, inseparable, and traceable only in retrospect, through the practices that institutions promulgate.

The main difference between Taylor and Castoriadis lies in their perception of and attention to the symbolic, and this has particular consequences. In an impressive survey spanning centuries and nations, Taylor in *Modern Social Imaginaries* tells the story of what he calls the long march of modernity, a tour-de-force history of the roots, beginnings, and perpetuations of Western civic and political societies as we know them today. It is important to note that he prefaces the book by saying that he focuses only on the modern social imaginary as this develops in the West, not on the trajectories of cultures and imaginaries other than the Western, which have necessarily resulted in other types of marches and modern social imaginaries. What, more specifically, is Taylor's modern social imaginary? A useful place to begin is with the distinction he makes between the social imaginary and social theory:

> I adopt the term imaginary (i) because my focus is on the way ordinary people "imagine" their social surroundings, and this is often not expressed in theoretical terms, but is carried in images, stories, and legends. It is also the case that (ii) theory is often the possession of a small minority, whereas what is interesting in the social imaginary is that it is shared by large groups of people, if not the whole society. Which leads to a third difference: (iii) the social imaginary is that common understanding that makes possible common practices and a widely shared sense of legitimacy.[17]

Herein is really contained the entirety of the social imaginary as what we may think of as enabling and enabled filter, from which Taylor then develops the account of the long march of Western modernity. The ingredients of any given imaginary of course vary, but in the case of the Western, modern social one, certain aspects are unyieldingly crucial: a new moral order deriving from emergent theories of natural law, which, first through Grotius and then through Locke, become the first building blocks for a normative contract between individuals "even prior to or outside of the political bond," and which rest on the idea that "human beings are rational, sociable agents who are meant to collaborate in peace to their mutual benefit."[18] What comes from this is radical: conceptions of legislative and governing legitimacy as handed down from time immemorial come into question, as does the hierarchical understanding of how members of a community relate to each other, and this rests on the questioning of similar ideas of order handed down from some unquestionable source of justification that lies above and beyond the community or culture.

The new moral order, Taylor goes on to state, is for the here and now rather than the ultimate (as a key to understanding reality), and if it is for the here and now, it may be either hermeneutic or prescriptive, something not yet realized but demanding to be integrally carried out. As the centuries progress the implications of this difference filter into more and more spheres of social life (property rights, gender roles, questions of equality, and so forth), and they travel, as Taylor puts it, along several axes, but finally order themselves as the background for a modern social imaginary that rests on the following understandings and their practices:

> (1) the order of mutual benefit holds between individuals (or at least moral agents who are independent of hierarchical orders); (2) the benefits crucially include life and the means to life, although securing these relates to the practice of virtue; and (3) the order is meant to secure freedom and easily finds expressions in terms of rights. To these we can add a fourth point:
>
> These rights, this freedom, this mutual benefit is to be secured to all participants equally. Exactly what is meant by equality will vary, but that it must be affirmed in some form follows from the rejection of hierarchical order.[19]

Among the revolutionary developments that ensue and that we, incorporated as we are in our modern social imaginary, perhaps do not realize, are the phenomenal effects of the new moral order and its social imaginary in terms of the "progress of disenchantment," the secularization of everyday life, the "disembedding, the eclipse of the world of magic forces and spirits."[20] The shift is an inevitable consequence of the new moral order, and it takes place in tandem with other modifications described earlier.

These are Taylor's main points of engagement with the relationship between imaginary and symbolism, understood here as centering on a kind of enchantedness that is cut off from rationalization and the new moral order that arranges agents in completely different relations and hierarchies. This difference between Taylor and Castoriadis is also the difference between their two projects: whereas Castoriadis elucidates the principles of the instituting imaginary of any society, across centuries and continents, Taylor specifically traces the trajectory of one such manifestation, the modern Western one. Thus, the idea of *embedding* figures as inherently enchanted, religious in a primary sense, serving as a moral compass that individuals and cultures abide by without self-consciously reflecting on it. Castoriadis is not oblivious to this: "A 'primitive' who would want to act not taking into account the distinctions between clans, a Hindu of the past who would decide to ignore the existence of the castes, would most likely be mad—or would soon become so." However, while this is part of Castoriadis's broader argument that we ourselves are incapable of letting go of our own imaginary as we peer into the past and therefore cannot help but apply the modern imaginary of ultimate rationalization to archaic societies, he does not view the form per se of past imaginaries as inherently distinct from the modern: "despite, or rather due to this extreme 'rationalization', the life of the modern world is just as dependent on the imaginary as any archaic or historical culture. What is presented as the rationality of modern society is simply a matter of form, externally necessary connections, the perpetual dominance of the syllogism."[21] Hence, disenchantment and magic not only do not figure in Castoriadis's work, the imaginary is a universal and inherent, if ever malleable, structure in which the formal underpinnings are constant, even if the content is not.

In one of the more interesting points of engagement between the two thinkers, it also follows that individuals are always embedded, or in Castoriadis's terminology, instituted. In Taylor's view, embeddedness is inherently linked to enchantment, to the sacred, or to magic, to a sense of self that is porous: "the enchanted world was one in which these forces could cross a porous boundary and shape our lives, psychic and physical. One of the big differences between us and them is that we live with a much firmer sense of the boundary between self and other. We are 'buffered' selves. We have changed."[22] We, the moderns, are a new kind of individual, placed among other individuals in new and very differently arranged constellations, and grounded in a rational conception of individualism (which means only a novel way of being an individual, not individualism in the common sense of the word). To this Castoriadis might retort that we are not essentially different, we are merely exponents and fragments of imaginaries that embed us (or institute us) differently, but that nevertheless embed us as thoroughly as any archaic society would. We are just not, in Taylor's language, enchantedly embedded anymore.

The American Master Imaginary

If it is true that we are entrenched in our own modern social imaginaries, how can we even begin to consider their gestalts in a remotely objective manner? For instance, as a Norwegian, I am quite aware that I, as one of the fragments of that particular imaginary, carry with me the traces of an understanding of a background and its practices that reach back to a peasant culture with rather unmodern habits. Those are small things, of course. The very fact that I can write that sentence makes me at the same time very much a modern, rational being—one of Taylor's buffered selves—capable of assuming a critical position outside the parameters of the imaginary to which I belong.

This leads, finally, to the specifically American social imaginary: could it be that the American one in certain crucial ways differs from its cousins in Europe? And, if that is so, is it possible that it has precisely to do with the kind of enchantment or magic to which I alluded initially? For it is not entirely true that the modern social imaginary rests only on the pragmatics of practices and understandings unhinged from their roots in a past embedded system and torn loose from great time in a narrow focus on the here and now. New sacred, symbolic references and spaces surely emerge; they are not necessarily grounded in religious time or origins but are symbolic and mythological nevertheless. More importantly, these emergent spaces are capable of building momentum as well as attaining features not entirely unlike the embedded structures of a not-too-distant past. The American imaginary comes trailing something that may paradoxically be situated precisely in what Taylor calls "time out of mind." This something has a mythological quality in that it presents itself as a symbolic structure over and above actual place, nation, or even people. Preceding the cultural nation's actualization are ideas of a utopia awaiting discovery and realization, and the combination of these two constitute an important reference point for what I have called the master imaginary. The mythical element in this can certainly be located in what Taylor refers to as "the story (or myth) of progress, one of the most important modes of narration in modernity," which the American most definitely shares with Europe.[23] But something else is at work here, too, and it resembles a more archaic, more traditional conception of order that has been handed down.

It bears repeating: America named an idea that long preceded its actual coming into being as the nation we know today. Djelal Kadir thus argues that "America" signifies an interesting tension between the "new land" that is "clear," "bright," "shining," "ever young," "ever fair," and "Nowhereland," a utopia, a place that is no place.[24] Perhaps we could say that it is when this myth merges with the emergent drive of a new moral order, which in the end leads to a new kind of individualism, that we get the contours of a potent imaginary specific to "America." It holds out the promise of progress and the unbridled pursuit of aspiration and potential happiness, and it spreads quickly into the world. It draws into its fold spaces far away, and it feeds and is fed by that part of imaginaries elsewhere that dreams of aspiration's free reign. This enables a distinction between, on the one hand, the bounded national space of the United States (the nation), and, on the other, the compelling attraction and signification within the modern social imaginary that the American one projects and finds projected back onto it in turn.

The already mythological or symbolic quality furthermore explains the unflinching perpetuation of this precise imaginary as we have witnessed it throughout past centuries. Also, precisely because it is a structure of signification residing in both the symbolic (myth) and the real (the instituted imaginary), it accounts for the spawning of a slew of minor, alternative imaginaries which the extreme interpretative flexibility of the master imaginary at once instantiates and subsumes under its particular and universally resonant tenor. And this is where the concept of the imaginary proves so useful as a tool of calibration: it enables the epistemological oscillation between the idea or ideal—the image *of*—on the one hand, and the "real" as it materializes in practices and understandings, on the other. If we compare this to the American dream, we see that the latter is a very different creature: not only is it not transferable to other societal structures, it is inherently a phantasm for individuals to pursue, not for societies to orchestrate and institute. It belongs firmly and only in the realm of symbolism, as the following example illustrates.

Hamilton Holt's seminal *Undistinguished Americans*, from 1906, is a collection of life-lets, stories "as told by themselves" recounting the realities of people from all kinds of social and ethnic stations in order to show the range of diversity (and injustices) in early-twentieth-century America. The first entry is "Life Story of a Lithuanian," where early on we find a passage in which the contrast between the conception of the dream and that of the imaginary, as well as the transition from the former to the latter, may be concretely observed. The Lithuanian is urged to leave his country for the United States by the traveling "shoemaker," a man who reads newspapers smuggled in from Germany about, among other things, the free country to the west, and who himself has a son living in Chicago. One night, having stopped by to mend some boots for the anonymous narrator's family, the shoemaker pulls out a paper on which his son has written something. It is a passage from the Declaration of Independence, which the son has been given in night school and has translated into Lithuanian for his father: "We know these are true things—that all men are born free and equal . . . that God gives them rights which no man can take away—that among these rights are life, liberty and the getting of happiness."[25] We notice the translation's slight alterations of the words, but it is the rendering of "pursuit" as "getting" that stands out. The meaning changes, it shifts the degree of attainability and the reality of the promise. "Pursuit" belongs to the realm of imagination and dreams, whereas the "getting" of happiness travels from this realm and over into that of the imaginary. The slippage marks the institution of the imagined into petrified fact, a thing of this world: once there, you will get happiness, which is very different from merely pursuing it.

The way the dream travels into the constitution of the imaginary in this example returns us to the principle from Bakhtin quoted earlier in this chapter: "every cultural act lives essentially on the boundaries, and it derives its seriousness and significance from this fact. Separated by abstraction from these boundaries, it loses the ground of its being and becomes vacuous, arrogant, it degenerates and dies." Essentially, what happens in the mistranslation of "pursuit" into "getting" is an act of transference on the boundary between a cultural outside and the inside of the American master imaginary, and the example consequently brings us back to the idea of going where one's advancement is, made possible by a hierarchy of moral order that finds a remarkable outlet in the New World. Taylor observes that in the United States

> Liberty is no longer simply belonging to the sovereign people, but personal independence. Moreover, this kind of liberty, generalized, is the necessary basis of equality, for it alone negates the older forms of hierarchical independence. What was seen in the old view as the source of self-centeredness, private interest, and corruption is now the driving force of a free and equal society.[26]

He concludes that "Independence is thus a social, and not just a personal, idea."[27] We see the Lithuanian correctly grasping the promise—the promise to dream. If we look at this more closely, the mistranslation is not a mistake as much as a transculturated affirmation of the contract between participants and the instituted and instituting grids of the master imaginary and its magic. The example from "Life Story of a Lithuanian" thus adds another layer to the dynamics of transference and can be read as a comment on a triangular gestalt of translation, transculturation, and transvaluation. Translation in this example echoes the longstanding tradition of translation as conversion and assimilation, discussed for instance by Walter Mignolo and Freya Schiwy in relation to missionaries in Latin America laboring for years on end to make available the Scriptures and grammars in Amerindian languages: "Translation was part of a project of transculturation, and transculturation was understood and described as 'conversion.' Today we would say assimilation."[28] In an echo of this description, the Lithuanian's case of "conversion" is inflected by the dialogue of transculturation, understood here as "an exchange between two cultures, both of them active, both contributing their share, and both co-operating to bring about a new reality."[29] For while translation may be fuelled by cultural and epistemological agendas that work to convert other agendas and bring them into one fold, in the Lithuanian's case the reciprocity involved in the "mis"-translation brings about an alternative valuation grounded in the slippage from pursuing to getting: this is the transvaluation that confirms even as it modifies the extended promise, but not to the extent that it questions its fundamental import. Between, on the one hand, the conceptualization of agents scattered across Europe awaiting their American destiny and destination, and, on the other, the dissemination of irresistible promise through differently constructed and founded epistemologies, conversion occurs as a semi-transvaluation. The process illustrates the obligation of the cultural inside of the imaginary to conduct a dialogue with and respond to its outsides, hinting at the potential for assimilation that reaches beyond the borders of actual place. As a spatial manifestation of what Doreen Massey refers to as "relations stretched out," the triad of translation, transculturation, and transvaluation anchors an agreement even from beyond the cultural sphere of the imaginary's participants.[30] Finally, what the story of the Lithuanian also illustrates is the distinction we can make between bounded national space—the United States—and the compelling attraction and signification that the American imaginary projects onto the world and finds projected back onto it in turn, thus ensuring the imaginary's perpetuation and continual renewal.

The chapters that follow have one overarching objective, namely to excavate, explore, and gauge the different refractions of and responses to the American imaginary. When we first turn to Drude Krog Janson's allowing her protagonist to negotiate the same contract of promise that we saw in the story of the Lithuanian, the similarities between the two narratives become obvious. However, *A Saloonkeeper's Daughter*, more profoundly and with compelling astuteness, also reflects Taylor's earlier point regarding independence as a social idea, one that arises uniquely in the context of the United States. Here is a truly modern story.

[2]

"PERPETUAL PROGRESS" IN DRUDE KROG JANSON'S *A SALOONKEEPER'S DAUGHTER*

DRUDE KROG JANSON'S novel *A Saloonkeeper's Daughter* was originally published in Minneapolis in 1887 with a similar-sounding title in Norwegian, *En Saloonkeepers Datter.*[1] The story of protagonist Astrid Holm's journey from Norway to late nineteenth-century America, moving from adolescence to adulthood and from failed actress to Unitarian minister, is a detailed and critical description of and from the Minneapolis of the 1880s that speaks to us across the centuries and contributes to our understanding of late-nineteenth-century Atlantic and American literary history. It is, however, only recently, more than a century later, that this story, coming from a Norwegian immigrant community in the American Midwest, has become available to a broader, English-reading audience. As Orm Øverland, who has edited and introduced the new edition, comments, "Drude Krog Janson is hardly a forgotten name in American literature: she fell into oblivion so rapidly that she seems never to have been noticed much in the first place."[2] She may not rank as a must-read, but since its restoration in 2002, her novel has secured a place among other recovered literary works.

A Saloonkeeper's Daughter lends itself to a number of different readings, and here I briefly sketch a few possible approaches.[3] One immediate focus is the role and revision of religious ideologies. The novel's representation of religion speaks to the tension between liberal religion and Norwegian Lutheranism in Norway, as well as its relationship to similar discussions in the United States, as much as it speaks to corresponding tendencies among the Norwegian immigrants in the American setting.[4] *A Saloonkeeper's Daughter* also reflects the intensifying relevance of the woman question and highlights the intimate transatlantic connections between women's movements in the United States and those on the European continent. In these contexts Astrid Holm and her journey toward maturity are also emblematic of more general cultural, political, and ideological tendencies and productions of her time.[5] And then, of course, we must remember that, when it was initially published, *A Saloonkeeper's Daughter* would most likely not have been considered American literature at all. Not only was it written in a language other than "Anglo-Saxon," it also pertains to that branch of literature commonly referred to as local color, the less-esteemed cousin of realism, and one that in general has been "marginalized by critics . . . for [its] focus on places outside the centres of literary power."[6] Naturally, this injustice has been righted in the past several decades, and the inclusion and appraisal of literatures formerly excluded from American literary history continue to create a deeper understanding of American literary and social history. We need only think of other restored works such as María Amparo Ruiz de Burton's *Who Would Have Thought It?* (1872) and *The Squatter and the Don* (1885), which both offer glimpses into the scarcely described realities of the newly annexed Mexicans of the American Southwest. Perhaps the most frightening example of local color's marginalization is Kate Chopin's now-classic *The Awakening*. While it is not aesthetically comparable to *The Awakening*, *A Saloonkeeper's Daughter* nevertheless finds a place in the pantheon of those works that survived the dusty repositories of oblivion.

However, the novels just mentioned have different geneses from that of *A Saloonkeeper's Daughter*; they were written in English by writers who resided permanently in the United States. By contrast, Drude Krog Janson, who had arrived with her children in Minneapolis in 1882 to join her husband, the priest and writer Kristofer Janson (at the time a household name both in Norway and in the Norwegian immigrant community in Minneapolis), did not stay. After her marriage came to an end, she decided to leave the United States in order to pursue her writing and personal independence back in Europe. This was in 1893, and Drude Krog Janson's life in America had lasted eleven years. And here is the curiosity I mentioned in chapter 1: Janson's novel is generally and without much comment assumed to be an American work. This is also echoed in the assessments by the translator Gerald Thorson and the editor Orm Øverland, who, along with other critics, classify it as such. Thorson comments that "Drawing on the realistic and literary movements in Europe and in America, Janson has written an American novel that anticipates the works of such writers as Theodore Dreiser, Stephen Crane, and Sarah Orne Jewett."[7] Øverland, a scholar specializing in Norwegian immigrant history and literature, has introduced and comprehensibly annotated the new edition. He appraises Janson's forgotten novel in the context of "American literatures in languages other than English": "One reason [Drude Krog Janson] has been neglected is the multilingual nature of American culture. Literary histories are silent on the fiction, drama, and poetry that came out of the late-nineteenth-century Midwest, partly because so much of it was in languages other than English." He goes on to observe that "For an important period of her life, she was an American writer. She can now be considered, in translation, for the distinctive qualities of her contribution to American literature."[8]

My own interest is not in whether or not *A Saloonkeeper's Daughter* is an American novel, because I fully agree that it is, and it is certainly not my intention to raise doubts thereof. The novel's status is connected to the concerns raised in the past couple of decades among scholars who painstakingly have undertaken the project of including non-English literatures in their American histories. Such inclusion necessarily also raises questions about what kind of processes of transculturation *cum* transvaluation accompany the belated arrivals on the shelves of American literature. While it is beyond the scope of this chapter to engage that problem in a comprehensive way, an excursion into one of its literary spaces may yield the contours of at least one route of elucidation. Hence my question about *A Saloonkeeper's Daughter*: What is going on in this novel that makes it American, even in Norwegian? For consider the novel's contexts: Drude Krog Janson spent a relatively short time in the United States; the narrative itself has few references to America as such and mostly takes place in "little Norway over there." Add to this that the novel was written in Norwegian for a

Norwegian-reading and Norwegian-speaking audience, and the question becomes rather insistent. As I explore in detail in what follows, the answer is intimately connected with the ideological impetus for and implications of the principle of the *Bildung* narrative, on the discursive, individual level but also, by extension, on the culturological one. I furthermore propose that if we focus on this particular genre as a way of seeing the world and its engagement with the American social imaginary, we can calibrate a very particular articulation of the latter at a specific time and place. At this intersection, between the principles of formation in *Bildung* and its carrying out of the American imaginary, lies a possible answer to why *A Saloonkeeper's Daughter* is an American novel.

It is really quite simple. There is in Janson's work a narrative orientation that we do not recognize from Norwegian literary imaginations of the same period (or any other, for that matter), and it can tentatively be described as a sensibility of the very *real* actualization of the promise of transformation, a sensibility that pertains to the New World. The element that makes *A Saloonkeeper's Daughter* unthinkable as a Norwegian novel is the complete and individual make-over the protagonist goes through, vaguely hinted at shortly before she embarks on her journey across the ocean: "In America she would begin to live again, and she dreamed of endless sun-lit plains where people were happy, where one could follow a call, and where no one treated others harshly because of prejudice."[9] Much could be said about these lines, but I draw particular attention to the quite remarkable echo of J. Hector St. John de Crèvecoeur's depictions of the "constitution" of Americans, approximately one hundred years earlier. In his third "Letter" he declares that "The Americans were once scattered all over Europe; here they are incorporated into one of the finest systems of population which has ever appeared, and which will hereafter become distinct by the power of the different climates they inhabit."[10] It is an oft-quoted sentence that may be taken to mean that those who are now Americans and residing within the borders of the United States were at one time dispersed everywhere. It can also, however, more interestingly be read as labeling people as "Americans" even prior to departure, identifying a precondition, a disposition, or an inherent potential that can only come to fruition and actualization once the move to the physical place has occurred: *Americans-in-becoming*, awaiting their incorporation into their destined and natural land. It seems inconceivable that a sentence of this magnitude and sheer magic attraction could originate in any other societal structure than one driven by "enchantment."

As we saw in chapter 1, the idea of America, coupled with a new conception of how humans live and interact, marks the contours of a very powerful version of what Charles Taylor defines as the modern social imaginary. It denotes, briefly speaking, a way of fitting together that is founded on ideas of the inherent rationality of the individual; a system of mutual benefit; and a thoroughly secular anchoring of society, its institutions, and the relationship between these and the people whom they seek to govern and guard. The argument, or rather, the long march of modernity, begins with the birth of a new moral order, which, Taylor says, "was most clearly stated in the new theories of Natural Law which emerged in the seventeenth century" by deriving "the normative order underlying political society from the nature of its constitutive members. Human beings are rational, sociable agents who are meant to collaborate in peace to their mutual benefit."[11] Of greatest relevance to the present discussion is what Taylor says about how an idea of our actually living together emerges gradually, through numerous adaptations and mutations. I quote the following at length, since it bears directly on the question of the Americanness of Janson's novel:

> The picture of society is that of individuals who come together to form a political entity against a certain preexisting moral background and with certain ends in view. The moral background is one of natural rights; these people already have certain moral obligations toward each other. The ends sought are certain common benefits, of which security is the most important.
>
> The underlying idea of moral order stresses the rights and obligations we have as individuals in regard to each other, even prior to or outside of the political bond. Political obligations are seen as an extension or application of these more fundamental moral ties. Political authority itself is legitimate only because it was consented to by

> individuals (the original contract), and this contract creates binding obligations in virtue of the preexisting principle that promises ought to be kept.[12]

In the reflections of both Crèvecoeur's "Letter" and Janson's protagonist Astrid, the "underlying idea of moral order" is already firmly in place, but it is geared toward a very particular space and direction that adds to Taylor's imaginary one crucial element: the utter rejection of things past and the embrace of the new, a contract informed by more than the secular, moral economy that would come to frame the West. The contract that *Americans-in-becoming* such as Astrid must enter into demands a future orientation with the individual as centerpiece, since only in such isolation can futurity be kept pure, as it were. Cultures of the communal, in order to stay so, must follow and abide by practices and habits formed by the collective (albeit always more or less under revision), as Astrid's reference to prejudices suggests. With the new land, dreamt into being before it was a reality, a very potent imaginary thus comes to fruition. While its birth as a nation is informed by similar processes as those leading up to the French Revolution, one element in particular causes this one imaginary to stand out. In Taylor's words, "Liberty is no longer simply belonging to the sovereign people, but personal independence. Moreover, this kind of liberty, generalized, is the necessary basis of equality, for it alone negates the older forms of hierarchical independence. . . . Independence is thus a social, and not just a personal, idea."[13] This is essentially the promise held out by the Declaration of Independence, but it is more than a promise. It also becomes an obligation in order to better serve the greater good.

Progress and the unbridled pursuit of aspiration and potential happiness thus come to canvass imaginations everywhere as an irresistible version of modernity, as they do to this day. The American imaginary draws into its fold spaces far away, and it both feeds and is fed by that part of imaginaries elsewhere that dream of aspiration's free reign, as indeed Astrid Holm dreams. As a consequence, we will see that her story is not really conceivable in a context where older orders still prevail. This is very clearly revealed through the genre in which her transformation into an American is accomplished. The generic mold interestingly replicates this very constituent of the American imaginary: the independent individual who is simultaneously socially bound. The *Bildung* genre as scaffolding or cast turns out to be a perfect vehicle for this design. One of its main ideological characteristics is, as Franco Moretti reminds us, the projection of "the biography of a young individual [as] the most meaningful viewpoint for the understanding and the evolution of history."[14] In narrating the story of the young immigrant girl and her journey toward maturity in the New World, the author taps into and describes a double movement in terms of an American tropological circumstance. The imaginary is both constitutive of and constituted by the participants' willingness to embrace this future-oriented, unfettered contract: individualism and personal independence as socialization into the larger society. In no small measure, this resonates with the ideology of the institutional frameworks that traditionally underlay the study of literature in the *Bildung* genre's place of birth, Germany. For, rather than being relegated to its own academic department, literature was instead "subsumed under the comprehensive discipline of *Germanistik*, the study, reinforcement, and transmission of the presumed cultural values of the nation. Thus, a question such as the definition of the Bildungsroman is an issue not confined to academic discourse, but spreads into the ideological self-understanding of the culture as a whole."[15]

In its origin, then, the convergence of narrating the self in relation to nation or society is embedded in generic requirements and a corresponding institutional confluence between a society's literature and culture. The bildungsroman works as a cast in a double fashion: it shapes from the outside, from the perspective of culture as overarching structure, into which its members are socialized and acculturated; and it shapes from the inside, as the protagonist aspires to the realization of herself or himself as an acculturated member of the community. As Richard Koselleck puts it, "It is characteristic of the German concept of Bildung that it recasts the sense of an upbringing offered from the outside (which still belongs to the concept during the eighteenth century) into the autonomous claim for a person to transform the world."[16]

The textual manifestations of the genre and the imaginary's working alongside each other and eventually merging begin early on in *A Saloonkeeper's Daughter*. Following the death of his wife, August Holm, a failed businessman from a well-off family in Kristiania (now Oslo), decides to immigrate to the United States. He tells his oldest daughter Astrid that "There a man with knowledge and experience can get ahead . . . I belong there where one is free of all this aristocratic nonsense." To Astrid the decision comes as something of a surprise, but she is quickly reconciled to the idea and agrees to join him after a year has passed. After all, she reflects, "there is much freedom there. Maybe there could be freedom for her, too."[17]

Astrid harbors a secret dream of becoming an actress, as her mother had been in her youth, and has spent her childhood and adolescence playacting with her mother's old costumes and reading every play she has been able to get her hands on. She is particularly taken with the character Hjørdis in Ibsen's play *The Vikings at Helgeland* (1857). Astrid's fascination with Hjørdis, who is commonly considered the forerunner of Ibsen's more famous female character Hedda Gabler of the play of the same name, indicates an early if unarticulated sense of independence and determination. To Astrid, immigrating to America opens up the possibility of pursuing her own dream of acting in front of people, not rats, as she used to do in the attic of her family's house in Norway. The contours of a trope are taking shape here, but they do not yet pertain to a uniquely American context. Astrid is simply reflecting the desire and dream embedded in all migratory projects, of creating a better life and a better future. To Astrid's father, America presents an escape from the humiliation of having failed at home, and the opportunity to start over again. His is the typical emigrant story, in which financial ruin is the main motivation for leaving. When Astrid, her younger brothers, and their nanny arrive a year later, it turns out that the "wine business" that her father has written and told them about in his letters is nothing fancier than a simple saloon regularly visited by other Norwegian immigrants. When she realizes the true nature of her father's business, Astrid despairs: "Dear God, dear God, . . . What shall I do? What shall I do?"[18]

The new beginning is thus framed by shame, for Astrid as well as for her father. To Mr. Holm, "it was a disgrace that he, a well-bred gentleman, the scion of an old patrician family, should sink so low." He takes comfort, however, in the fact that "none of his old acquaintances and friends saw him in these circumstances."[19] We see here that the novel's discourse has not left the imaginary and auxiliaries of the old country and the past, and that the potential and promise of the new imaginary are not yet available. We could perhaps rephrase this and suggest that the filter through which the participants are seen and through which they themselves see is not yet accessible and hence cannot provide their constitution into the imaginary's "conversation" as enabled participants in the game.

Immigrant literature generally displays a narrative oscillation between the potential of the future and nostalgia for the past. Past and present coexist uneasily in a complex space of simultaneity, and it is ultimately left to the immigrant alone to find her way out of this confusion. This is also true of Astrid Holm. From that point in the story that has just been described, the narrative of the protagonist's coming of age alternates between unbridled enthusiasm for the possibilities she sees lying ahead and acute bouts of homesickness, disgust, and disillusion with her new environment and life. An incident that takes place not long after Astrid's arrival illustrates this dialectic. Urged on by her suitor Meyer, she agrees to act in a play, which also pleases her father, who sees a way out of his own mire by attempting to find his daughter a suitable and respectable husband. Astrid is happy, dreaming as she still does of following her calling to become an actress. The play is by Bjørnstjerne Bjørnson, a famous Norwegian writer who will assume a critical role toward the end of the novel.[20] The play, however, turns out to be a mere excuse for a dance and a beer brawl orchestrated by Mr. Holm and his business interests, and Astrid's disappointment and repugnance at the audience's vulgarity and disregard for the play itself all but crush her. She realizes how naïve she has been, and there and then abandons her dreams of the theater. When the play is over, she unhappily joins the others in drinking and dancing. The evening ends with her getting sick, from alcohol as well as the disgust and horror at Meyer's making inappropriate passes at her. The incident throws

Astrid into a fever and also changes something inside her. The following passage marks the first turning point, or moment of crisis, in the *Bildung* process:

> When Astrid got out of bed the day after, she was well again. Anyone looking at her closely, though, would have noticed that those two days had brought about a great change. Something cold, almost stony, had come over her. Her blood-red mouth now had a firm and determined look. She had buried her childhood with its happy memories, her bright youth with its jubilant premonitions, dreams and hopes.[21]

The conventions of the *Bildung* genre demand such moments of crisis, and typically they function as episodes of potential meaning: "The novelistic episode is almost never meaningful in itself. It becomes so because someone—in the Bildungsroman usually the protagonist—gives it meaning."[22] These are, in other words, encounters with the surrounding world that potentially and eventually will constitute the protagonist's final *Bildung*. In Astrid's case, however, the real meaning of her submission to societal norms is only revealed later, in a second moment of crisis. Before that, she agrees to become engaged to the well-respected lawyer Mr. Smith. When he asks her to be his wife and tries to kiss her, she reacts very much as she did when Meyer tried to kiss her. She faints, and only when she arrives home safely do we realize how desperately unhappy she is: "what had become of her in this one year? A tearless woman who with a bitter smile walked toward her humiliation."[23] Astrid's father is of course delighted with the prospect of marriage and fails to note that his daughter, like Dame Margit in Astrid's favorite Ibsen play, *The Feast at Solhaug*, marries out of resignation, not love.

Astrid's acquiescence to marrying Smith, however unhappy the prospect may be, fulfils an important requirement. The *Bildung* genre traditionally demands that the protagonist comply with the wishes and expectations of society and family—in this lies the pedagogical lesson. The entire purpose of the crisis is to have the hero choose which path to follow, and this choice must be one that ideally marks, as Walter Sokel puts it, "the utopian synthesis of individuality and socialization." True to form, then, *The Saloonkeeper's Daughter* centers on the individual's negotiation of the dichotomy between autonomy and socialization in such a fashion that the individual's formation at least seems to "[coincide] without rifts with one's social integration as a simple part of the whole."[24] In Astrid's case, her agreement to marry the unsympathetic but solvent and socially acceptable Smith signifies this integration and synthesis. For the *Bildung* process is not entirely complete and the ending is not entirely happy without marriage. An unsurpassed "metaphor for the social contract" in the bildungsroman tradition, marriage stands for far more than the agreed bond between two individuals; it is also the ultimate contract between the individual and the world.[25] Astrid's decision puts her father at peace and satisfies Smith as well as the expectations of society. The community of mostly Norwegian immigrants applauds her finally coming to her senses: "Everywhere she was received with open arms and a friendly smile. . . . All were delighted to see the 'sweet Miss Holm.'"[26]

Just as Astrid's fate seems sealed and the date for the wedding has been set, Bjørnson himself arrives in town to give a lecture. To Astrid, "It was as if everything was torn up in her again just at hearing that Bjørnson was coming to town. . . . Now in her humiliation, when she had given up everything, he was coming. What should that mean? If he had only come a year earlier, then, perhaps, he could have saved her. Now it was too late." The lecture and subsequent personal meeting with Bjørnson will mark the second moment of crisis in Astrid's *Bildung*. To hear him speak fills her with joy, "a new sense of faith," but one that quickly dissipates when she goes home to the rooms above the saloon: "It was impossible for her to be saved."[27] The next evening, however, she is introduced to Bjørnson at a dinner party. Against the pact with Smith and society, a life led as possession, Bjørnson emerges as a powerful reminder of a life led in and by faith. The meeting awakens Astrid, who then writes a note to Smith telling him the marriage is off, and, despairing at the predicament she is in, goes to see Bjørnson in private to seek his advice. The most significant lesson that crystallizes from their conversation is the poet's warning that Astrid not bow down to conventions:

> "A woman in our day has no excuse if she gives up," said Bjørnson firmly. "God forbid! That time is past, especially here in America. Here a defeated woman does not have to take her own life or give herself in an immoral marriage, that is no better than another form of prostitution. That is the history of barbaric ages and it has demanded millions of sacrifices. Now that must come to an end."[28]

Bjørnson here voices a conception that pits old world and New World against each other in a dialectical pairing in which the former is barbaric and past, the latter civilized and new. It is quite intriguing that a Norwegian, not an American, projects this view, and Bjørnson here breaks with standard mores in both Norway and the United States at the time. However, Øyvind Gulliksen argues that Janson here lets Bjørnson carry ideas that he may not have had in real life, but that the American context of the novel made possible. Gulliksen, moreover, concludes that "*A Saloonkeeper's Daughter* is a novel of religious thought, inspired by the new liberalism of Bjørnstjerne Bjørnson, the Norwegian poet, and a testing in fiction of Unitarian views in the New England tradition of William E. Channing."[29] This is a compelling point, which further strengthens the idea that the novel remains, even at this late point in the narrative, steeped in moral and cultural outlooks that have not yet been "enabled," adapted and transformed into primers of the American imaginary, although they are now close.

Bjørnson's final advice to the unhappy and confused Astrid is that she become a minister, "a minister like those found here in America—gentle, loving, men and women who proclaim peace on earth, who do not believe that people are little devils created for hell's fire. Instead, they have a glowing faith in the victory of goodness in the world and in perpetual progress."[30] At this point it becomes clear that Astrid's fulfilling of the *Bildung* ideal, by agreeing to marriage and the demands represented by the *Bildung* framework, is valid only in the context of one part of the society that she is acculturating into, namely the Norwegian-American community. As I said initially, the novel makes few references to sources or events outside this enclave, and as Astrid has painfully come to experience, the traces of an imaginary whose social institutions and expectations remain entrenched in an older temporality still hold sway. We can read the two moments of crisis, therefore, as necessary discursive and strategic nodes for the projection of personal and cultural transformation.

For it is the second moment of crisis, with Bjørnson as catalyst, that marks Astrid's true conversion, in more senses of the word than one. We return here to the idea of genres as forms of seeing and interpreting the world, as structural molds or grids. The transition from one model of *Bildung* to another is not antithetical to generic conventions; instead it echoes the very nature of any genre as never finalized. As Mikhail Bakhtin reminds us, genre "lives in the present, but always *remembers* its past, its beginnings. Genre is a representative of creative memory in the process of literary development. Precisely for this reason is genre capable of guaranteeing the *unity* and *uninterrupted continuity* of this development."[31] It is this transference from one imaginary to another that the two moments of crisis together project, also thereby convincingly refracting Astrid's conversion from *American-in-becoming* to enabled participant.

The decision Astrid now makes stands out in American literary history. After a few days in the home of her father, she announces that she is leaving for good: "Astrid walked hurriedly up the street, never looking back."[32] She then seeks out Helene Nielsen, a female doctor she has met on occasion and found sympathy from. Here she finds a haven:

> "You have severed all ties?" There was deep joy in [Helene's] voice. "And you come to me? Then I haven't lived in vain when the unfortunate and forlorn turn to me. This is the happiest moment of my life. It makes up for many, many disappointments. . . . You have no idea how I have been drawn to you ever since the first time I saw you. Oh, how it cut my heart when I saw you being destroyed. Yes, you would have been destroyed if you hadn't broken it off. But now all will be well."[33]

The path Astrid chooses reverses and invalidates her first path in a final act of rejection and withdrawal from society. Her refusal is further augmented by the fact that she chooses to live with another woman. Janson does not fail to give this aspect due notice: "Thus did these two women, who had both left their places in society, make a pact for life."[34] The companionship is not in itself unheard of in American literature, and as Axel Nissen shows, "Janson's novel relates to and intersects with a similar rhetoric of gender in works by authors such as Maria Cummins, Sarah Orne Jewett, William Dean Howells and Henry James." Where the story of Astrid's coming of age *is* unique, however, is in its denouement: "None of the main female characters die. None of the main female characters marry. And the two romantic friends, the novel strongly suggests, will live happily ever after."[35] The radical break with the established backdrop pertaining to gender roles does not mean Janson's representation detracts from the master trope of the American imaginary, for it is Astrid's found freedom to pursue her own interpretation of it that prevails in the narrative, not really her romantic friendship with Helen. The imaginary has not lost its power to engender other, new participants in its conversation, and it is at this juncture that Astrid's trajectory analogizes the real marvel of the trope: the promise of unbridled aspiration can be pursued over and over again, by means of new members who join to participate. This moment in the novel thus also illustrates what Charles Taylor suggests about the dynamism of the modern social imaginary in general, namely that "the relation between practices and background understanding is therefore not one-sided. If the understanding makes the practice possible, it is also true that it is the practice that largely carries the understanding."[36] In a case such as the American one, these practices are differently informed precisely because "background understandings" stem from a slew of different, old-world imaginaries. Hence the carrying of practices leaves behind residues that, in the encounter with the master trope, respond in a variety of ways. Astrid's case is thus not unique, but in leaving no scar in the rift between old and new, her conversion illustrates an extreme model of conversion to the pursuit of one's own happiness. Sacvan Bercovitch's comment in relation to the privileging of opposition as personal radicalism applies to this model, for "whether the choice is the right to live or the rights of dissent, and whether (as a dissenter) you say 'No in thunder' or 'I would prefer not to,' subjectivity is reified as the 'I' of eternity, like the eye of

God on the dollar bill."[37] (I will come back to this proposition in chapter 6.)

I mentioned other recovered and regional literary works earlier, and it may be useful to revisit *The Squatter and the Don* in order to gauge with precision alternative outcomes to the one we are dealing with here. Ruiz de Burton wrote that novel in the same period as Janson wrote hers, and to an extent it refracts some of the same generic elements, in particular the melodramatic, discursive sentiment and the traits of the roman à clef: *The Squatter and the Don* is set in California, it engages explicitly and at times crucially with historical and political events of its period, and includes references to real-life participants, notably the "Big Four" (Collis Huntington, Leland Stanford, Charles Crocker, and Mark Hopkins, who were mainly responsible for building the Central Pacific Railroad and California's railroad system between 1861 and 1900). The differences, however, are still greater than such similarities. Most significantly, *The Squatter and the Don*'s narrative orientation never compromises the ideological and discursive grounding it retains in a different past, a period when California was still Mexican and the Don a real Don. Ruiz de Burton's novel thus occupies a position in the cultural-discursive border space that opened up after the Mexican-American War of 1848, and it comes down to us as an early articulation of the dialogic exchange of the borderland. In this it also lodges itself firmly within a different strand in the American literary tradition, namely that which comes with a hyphen, in this case "Mexican-American." These two components mark the currents that inform the discursive product, not as conversion, but as persevering negotiation of the encounter with the imaginary.

This is not so in *A Saloonkeeper's Daughter*. In the seven months that follow Astrid's meeting with Bjørnson, she assists Helene in her work and devotes the rest of her time to studying English and history. Much of the misery she sees on house calls with her friend is caused by drunkenness, and she decides to give a public lecture on temperance. The attempt fails when the crowd, cheered on by Meyer, drowns her speech in loud remarks regarding her background: "Away with the saloonkeeper's wench!" The experience leaves Astrid in a state of hopelessness, feeling that she will never be able to shed her past, no matter what choice she makes: "Wherever I turn," she tells Helene, "my past follows me."[38]

It is difficult at this point in the novel to see how the protagonist's second moment of crisis might generate anything but withdrawal, far removed from the contract with society that would fulfill the generic requirements of crisis and the pedagogy of choosing correctly. And yet, the resolution that now ensues turns isolation and rejection into precisely that, a contract and a path that are culturally, aesthetically, and socially acceptable. For after the bitter disappointment at the temperance lecture, which is in many ways a repetition of the episode of the play, Helene advises Astrid to leave town and begin her training as a Unitarian minister in Pennsylvania. And so it is that Astrid receives an audience after all. The transformation progresses from following a calling of the secular to that of the sacred, from despair to hope, from confusion to clarity, from adolescence to maturity, and, most importantly, from Norwegian immigrant to enabled American. If the protagonist's moments of crisis gain significance only in the fullness of time, then it is now that we see the true meaning of Astrid's journey. As it turns out, her final choice brings her a peace of mind and a sense of self that are in fact recognized through her ordination as a minister. The very last lines of the novel read: "Now she saw before her a sea of friendly faces, tear-filled eyes, as all welcomed her and waited, quietly and expectantly, to hear what she had to say. . . . She was at home here. She had not mistaken her call. She had reached her destination." The utopian synthesis between individual and society is consequently no longer utopian, and before Astrid lies a future that may still be "veiled in uncertainty and mystery," but one that must yield to her faith in the self's power to overcome those very uncertainties.[39]

The contract between self and society is furthermore based on a very specific trope, namely what Bjørnson calls "perpetual progress," and it is what connects the path of the individual with that of society at large. For the novel's denouement also speaks directly to the culturological setting for Astrid's *Bildung*, namely the *Bildung* of the nation itself, along with its social imaginary. In leaving behind "degraded" Minneapolis to become a minister somewhere out

West, Astrid emulates the grand design embedded in the perpetual: the idea of the everlasting clean slate and new beginnings, forever stretching into the future, Bercovitch's newness as a "continual movement toward endings that issues in an endless affirmation of beginnings."[40] Astrid's personal journey toward maturity and completion merges with the culturological master trope of the New World. Conversations and experiences converge and are finally given meaning, and the protagonist chooses without suffering a debilitation of self.

Finally, the second moment of crisis may be seen as a literal as well as metaphorical act of conversion that, on the individual and personal level, replicates the larger culturological context. Herein lies the connection between Bjørnson's "perpetual progress" and the reason why we read *A Saloonkeeper's Daughter* as an American novel. Following the second crisis, the narrative discourse changes and refracts an orientation of faith in the new self and the newly found mission that resonates with the design of the burgeoning nation. Having recovered from the Civil War and experiencing tremendous economic and demographic growth, the United States in this period confirms its position as site for the aspiration of individual and cultural coming into being, and destination of unprecedented immigration. Of equal importance, both energies are consolidated and confirmed as virtuous in and of themselves, corresponding to the paradoxical redaction of the modern social imaginary as personal independence that is socially beneficial. This confirmation constitutes and is constituted by a culturological orientation that embraces present and future potential rather than the past and its nostalgia. David Lowenthal remarks:

> In severing imperial bonds, Americans discarded not only the mother country but many of its traditions. Three interrelated ideas helped justify dismissal of the past: a belief that autonomy was the birthright of each successive generation; an organic analogy that assigned America to a place of youth in history; and a faith that the new nation was divinely exempt from decay and decline.[41]

In Astrid's personal journey and severing of bonds with the past, her choice is consistent with that of society. Her gaze, as that of the culture she is becoming a part of, is directed not toward the homes left behind on the other side of the Atlantic but toward the future, represented in this case by the American West. The night before Astrid leaves she tells Helene, "My body belongs to me, and no one else has a right to it. Just think! I am saved." Her salvation comes about through religiosity, but within an American context in which religion is transformed into the empowerment of the individual—in relation to herself and to society as much as to God. Astrid goes into the future, and as the novel ends there is no indication of her looking back. She will "go west and take over an American congregation,"[42] and the past indeed becomes a foreign country.

Drude Krog Janson's narrative is so emblematically American that it stands as an ideal template for the kinds of encounters with the American master imaginary that are so often handed down to us. Moreover, the protagonist-individual in her own personal story allegorizes the very constitution and institution of the modern social imaginary's disembedding and dehierarchization of its participants or members into a different arrangement of ideas of equality, liberty, and what Taylor refers to as mutual benefits. Øverland's statement, quoted at the beginning of this chapter, that "for a period of her life Drude Krog Janson was an American writer," now seems beyond doubt an accurate assessment, and it is also worth noting that the text in and of itself comes to stand as testimony to the American imaginary as enabling filter. In the course of the eleven years Janson spent in Minneapolis, she internalized practices and understandings to such a degree that she was able to refract them, very precisely, as a cultural conversion carried by generic as well as ideological conventions and grids. What she tapped into was a template for individual and culturological self-fashioning that had already been scripted into existence by, among others, the national bard Walt Whitman.

Astrid Holm's turn of spirit comes after Whitman's magic, as do all the other texts in the present selection, and chronologically as well as thematically, it may seem a little backward not to let Whitman lead and the other readings follow. However, the sheer immensity of Whitman's aesthetic and ideological outlook may be better gauged after we have seen in Drude Krog Janson the actualization of the imaginary. Secondly, Astrid's story is only *one* story, for advancement is not for all, as we know all too well, and performances and interpretations do not always accept and fit so neatly onto the scripted expectations.

[3]

SONGS OF DIFFERENT SELVES: WHITMAN AND GONZALES

SOCIAL IMAGINARIES CARRY particular expectations to their participants. These are disseminated in various ways, commonly through customs and traditions, which teach members the necessary enabled and enabling filters. Founding cultural documents are among the pillars of such traditions, including literary canons that measure how a culture conceptualizes its provenance, genesis, purpose, and indeed, essence, not only for itself but, just as importantly, for others. Walt Whitman's "Song of Myself" is a remarkable founding document in this respect: it is carried by and also carries forth the currents of the American imaginary in its most tropologically compelling form. It creates figures, forms, and images that to this day remain vital to the cultural grids according to which the imaginary's members interpret and perform their participation. As a founding document "Song of Myself" can furthermore be read as a scripted schema that in a sense choreographs other performances of its mythological template. Regarding the relationship between Walt Whitman and the American nation, Benjamin Barber thus observes that:

> [Whitman] is an American emblematic as Voltaire and Sartre might be thought of as French emblematics, or Goethe and Kant as German emblematics, or Tolstoy and Dostoevsky as Russian emblematics. When we think about America, we think of Walt Whitman, and when we think about Walt Whitman we think of America—though this may also be to think about what America is not or about how other places are, in certain ways, also American.[1]

While I personally do not always think about Whitman when I think about America, I see Barber's point, partly because there is an element here that closely resembles the assumption about *A Saloon-keeper's Daughter* as inherently American. More relevant, though, is the flip side that Barber points to, namely that to think about Whitman and America is just as often to think about what they are *not*, how the equation does not always work.

When we line up Rodolfo "Corky" Gonzales's equally foundational and epic but lesser-known poem "I am Joaquín," which dates from 1967, alongside "Song of Myself," such alternative vistas certainly open up. "I am Joaquín" does not arrange itself according to the master imaginary and its institutions' figures. Instead, its restoration of Chicano history is firmly rooted in a different kind of "mode and a form of social-historical doing," in the words of Cornelius Castoriadis, as "creation and ontological genesis in and through individuals' doing and representing/saying," which are in turn "instituted historically."[2] In this sense, "institution," to briefly recapitulate Castoriadis's definition, is obviously not "social security or a mental health clinic. We are speaking, first and foremost, about language, religion, and power, and about what the individual is in a given society." Foundational documents, as fragments of the enabling filter, or as fragments of the institution, are immensely important in this respect: "[The] institution provides 'meaning' for socialized individuals, but it also supplies them with the resources for bringing this meaning into existence for themselves," Castoriadis says later on. Of more relevance to the context of canonical founding documents, he also states: "What [artists'] imagination sires acquires a 'real'—that is, social-historical—existence, and it does so by using an infinitude of means and elements—language, to begin with—that the artist could never have created 'all by herself.'"[3] I do not argue that Gonzales's poem responds self-consciously to Whitman's "Song of Myself" in the same way that, say, Langston Hughes's "I, Too" engages directly with "I Sing America." However, "I am Joaquín" displays enough remarkable structural similarities to, and, indeed, what seem to be overt borrowings from, "Song of Myself" to allow a reading of the two as participants in, or fragments of, the same dialogue.

There is an additional incentive to comparatively gauging the imaginary's representation in the two works. Gonzales tends to be left out of the substantial intertextual company Whitman keeps and has been assigned to. For instance, Gonzales does not figure in Kirsten Gruesz's interesting exploration of Whitman as a Latino poet, despite the fact that: "The list of contemporary U.S. Latino poets who address Whitman more or less directly in their writing is startlingly long and inclusive—from the *caribeños* Martín Espada, Victor Hernández Cruz, and Julia Alvarez to Jimmy Santiago Vaca, to the Colombian born pop songstress Shakira."[4] Hopefully, the inclusion of Gonzales in this pantheon will add to our readings of both him and Whitman, this "kosmos, of Manhattan the son,"[5] and illuminate how the social imaginary as it was scripted in Whitman's master template comes with oversights and blind spots predicated on its role in and as a "form of social-historical doing" that enables as much as it deters.

Whitman and "Everything"

One of the striking characteristics of Walt Whitman's poetry, for new as well as old readers, is the unremitting fusion of the self with any imaginable entity outside that self, into long, at times nearly endless catalogues of synecdochic orchestrations. Such constellations of parts and wholes are announced by the poet himself in "Starting from Paumanok": "I will not make poems with reference to parts, / But I will make poems, songs, thoughts, with reference to ensemble."[6] There is, however, another kind of equalizing at work, a poetic, temporal orientation that persistently gravitates toward the futurizing present. When the poetic eye occasionally does gaze into the past, it is to collapse that past into the present moment and space of poetic utterance. A typical example of this is "Section 33" from "Song of Myself," which introduces the subsequent catalogue, nearly ten pages long, with an invocation precisely of temporal and spatial collapse and, indeed, absolution: "My ties and ballasts leave me." This liberation from the grids of time and space sets the poet "afoot with [his] vision," after which follow a slew of visitations to places "by the city's quadrangular houses—in log huts, camping /

with lumbermen," and to a range of types (skipper, martyr, slave, fireman, artillerist), all of whom the poet "is." All this culminates in the line toward the end of the section: "I take part, I see and hear the whole." The making uniform spatial as well as temporal multiplicities is sifted through a relationship of parts and whole that is the recurrent structure throughout. Interestingly, however, in the section that follows "Section 33," we hear of the fall of the Alamo, or rather, of what the poet "knew in Texas" in his youth: "(I tell not the fall of Alamo, / Not one escaped to tell the fall of Alamo, / The hundred and fifty are dumb yet at Alamo)."[7] One could conceivably connect this detail to Whitman's stance on the war between the United States and Mexico that followed Texas's independence in 1835 and its subsequent entry into the United States as the twenty-eighth state. As editor of the *Brooklyn Eagle*, he was an ardent supporter of this war, and the tone and outlook of his editorials to that effect are certainly radically different from those of his poetry:

> Yes: Mexico must be thoroughly chastised! . . . We are justified in the face of the world, in having treated Mexico with more forbearance than we have ever treated an enemy—for Mexico, though contemptible in many respects, is an enemy deserving a rigorous "lesson." . . . Let our arms now be carried with a spirit which shall teach the world that, while we are not forward a quarrel, America knows how to crush, as well as how to expand!"[8]

The sentiments reflected here could account for the consignment of the battle of the Alamo in "Song of Myself" to a depository, not to be mentioned again, in a kind of interring of what the poet on behalf of national sentiment perceives as a historical injustice and tragedy that his otherwise all-encompassing log cannot accommodate.

This is the exception, however, and I now turn in more detail to the implications of the equalizing of each and every person, and more specifically to the invitation and, in some cases, the directive to the addressee to pursue his or her own version of America. As the poet announces in "One's Self I Sing": "Of Life immense in passion, pulse, and power, / Cheerful, for freest action form'd under the laws divine, / The Modern Man I sing."[9] These lines are already the unheard articulation of a New World–view, a powerful instantiation of a new social arrangement, as an expression of what Castoriadis calls a new "mode and form of social-historical doing."[10] In other words, the compass for Whitman's refracting of self and society may be linked to the progression of a new moral order. As outlined in chapter 1, what Taylor calls the new order rearranges individuals, out of their placements within embedded and enchanted hierarchies outside which no one can stand, into an increasingly expansive understanding of society as "that of individuals who come together to form a political entity against a certain preexisting moral background and with certain ends in view. The moral background is one of natural rights; these people already have certain moral obligations towards each other." This radical shift from enchanted to disenchanted societal ordering does not mean, however, that God is dead: "rather, [the ideal order] was designed by God, an order in which everything coheres according to God's purposes."[11] The prerequisites that Taylor here delineates can be related to Whitman's exultations in his call for the "freest action form'd under the laws divine," for "divine" here must be understood not as divinity handed down and accepted mindlessly, "time out of mind," but as divinity residing in and defined as the wellspring of human essence as God-inspired and good, in a spiritual sense but also, importantly, in a pragmatic and human sense. This variation on the divine is, after all, also connected to the various understandings and redactions of self-reliance.

The development of Taylor's modern social imaginary and the spreading of a new arrangement into more and more niches of civil and political life could proceed more freely in the New World than in the old. The reason, as Taylor suggests, is that in Europe (and in other places), the dissemination of a new political and civic imaginary takes place "partly through the crystallization of a class imaginary of subordinate groups, particularly workers."[12] The notion of class as a category of collective self-understanding refers to the classical European tradition of labor unions, and its absence as an anchor for ranking individuals within a larger system has tremendous implications for identity politics in the New World. With class eliminated as a category having the potential to transcend ethnicity, gender, and race, personal independence as socially beneficial is a logical outcome. We already saw this transcendence powerfully demonstrated in Astrid Holm's two moments of crisis: empowered, or "enabled" to rid herself of past "crystallizations," Astrid freely pursues her own destiny in the drive for both personal and social happiness.

Moreover, Whitman's spatial collapse of American types and scenes, the synecdochic choreography of everyone into a single temporal and spatial moment—"ties and ballasts" left behind—at least in part accounts for why we may find here the richest and fullest expression of the American imaginary as it institutes itself at a relatively early point in the social history of the United States. The insistent, forward-looking gaze of "Song of Myself" contributes to the tropological sanctioning and blueprint for an enduring, specifically American imaginary torn loose from old hierarchies and embeddings. It may even serve as a bridgehead from the sociohistorical moment of writing (of social doing) to an aesthetic articulation of the nation. The register of forms and figures extends in gravitation and attraction well beyond the second half of the nineteenth century, and they all, ultimately, center on the promises of aspiration and futurity as ideals of personal and social adjustment and success in a specific performance of democracy.

Of course, Whitman did not emerge out of a void, and Ralph Waldo Emerson is generally credited with bringing Whitman to the fore. The lecture that eventually became known as "The Poet" affected Whitman the most significantly: "I was simmering, simmering; Emerson's words brought me to a boil," as he famously recalled. And it is easy to see the influence of the one man on the other; the monumental body of scholarly work on the relationship testifies to it. Next, I quickly place Emersonian transcendentalism in its context as a uniquely American ideological and philosophical expression of the modern social imaginary and briefly rehearse Emerson's call for an American, poetic voice. Both are crucial nodes in an evolving culturological schema of identification and reference against which Whitman and the imaginary may be fruitfully appreciated.

Many consider Emerson the first American philosopher proper, himself an author of founding documents. His rather idiosyncratic, transcendental outlook, which stressed self-reliance and a sense of spirituality inspired by the East, served as the center of American intellectual life from the 1830s to the Civil War, leaving behind deep-seated influences well into our own time. In Emerson's own words, the main tenets of his ideological stance are as follows:

> What is popularly called Transcendentalism among us, is Idealism. As thinkers, mankind have ever divided into two sects, Materialists and Idealists; the first class founding on experience, the second on consciousness; the first class beginning to think from the data of the senses, the second class perceive that the senses are not final, and say, the senses give us representations of things, but what are the things themselves, they cannot tell. The materialist insists on facts, on history, on the force of circumstances, and the animal wants of man; the idealist on the power of Thought and of Will, on inspiration, on miracle, on individual culture.[13]

It is not hard to find the echoes of the privileging of transcendental idealism in Whitman's work, but neither are Emerson's words conceivable outside the new moral order and the path that it took in America: he too spoke from inside the budding imaginary. It rested precisely on the transcendentalist "power of Thought and of Will, on inspiration, on miracle, on individual culture," which Whitman transformed into a schema for limitless cultural transference combined with praiseworthy individualism. The directive to "no longer take things at second or third hand, nor look through / the eyes of the dead, nor feed on the spectres in books," to "listen to all sides and filter them for your self," anticipates and resonates with Astrid Holms's turn of spirit and decision to go west in pursuit of her own dreams and future, and it continues to generate adaptations and derivations, across centuries and continents.[14]

In a thoroughly horizontal outlook and a narrative orientation that accommodated difference within the great fold, Whitman sounded marching orders for a national cultural narrative uniquely capable of transference. But more than that, he sang the self into the fabric without rifts, without seams, and the song was carried in a mold that sprouted from the American imaginary itself, as did the poet himself. Again, Emerson had something to do with this:

> We have yet had no genius in America, with tyrannous eye, which knew the value of our incomparable materials, and saw, in the

> barbarism and materialism of the times, another carnival of the same gods whose picture he so much admires in Homer; then in the middle age; then in Calvinism. Banks and tariffs, the newspaper and caucus, methodism and unitarianism, are flat and dull to dull people, but rest on the same foundations of wonder as the town of Troy, and the temple of Delphos, and are as swiftly passing away. Our logrolling, our stumps and their politics, our fisheries, our Negroes, and Indians, our boasts, and our repudiations, the wrath of rogues, and the pusillanimity of honest men, the northern trade, the southern planting, the western clearing, Oregon, and Texas, are yet unsung. Yet America is a poem in our eyes; its ample geography dazzles the imagination, and it will not wait long for metres.[15]

The enumerations that filled pages and pages in Whitman's project of writing the nation and all its constituent parts resound stylistically as well as ideologically with the passage above. "Song of Myself" and its lists of places, professions, beings, emotions, traditions, and creeds are all collapsed into the master trope of self as all-encompassing, predicated on miracle and will of thought. "Section 15" is one of the better illustrations of this. Whitman shows us glimpses and types from everyday American life in a catalogue that runs over two and one-half pages, ending with the lines: "And these tend inward to me and I tend outward to them, / And such as it is to be of these more or less I am, / And of these one and all I weave the song of myself."[16] The distinction that Castoriadis makes between the image *of* something and the imaginary as unceasing production of "*figures/ forms/images*, on the basis of which alone there can ever be a question of something," is worth reconsidering here.[17] Whitman represents both: His poetry is an image *of*, an emblem precisely in the sense of image, the ornamental, a likeness, but not the thing in itself. At the same time, out of this likeness is created and instituted a vast repertory of figures, which in turn have been re-created, adapted, and revisited as figures and forms intimately linked to the nation, to the nation's imagining of itself, and to its imaginary, which is continually developing yet in some ways unchanging. Moreover, in its presentation of both the image and the imaginary, Whitman's poetics can be linked meaningfully to what Taylor calls "new modes of narration":

> [The] new collective subject, a people or a nation that can found its own state, that has no need for a previous action-transcendent foundation, needs new ways of telling its story. . . . The sense that the present, postfounding order is right has to be expressed in terms that consort with this [secular] understanding of time. We can no longer describe it as the emergence of a self-realizing order lodged in higher time. The category that is at home in secular time is rather that of growth, maturation, drawn from the organic realm. A potential within nature matures.[18]

The catalogues, the organicism, the enumerations that drove D. H. Lawrence mad, the collapse of constituent parts into an "ensemble" and of heterochronism into one single, future-oriented, expanding moment, are all constitutive of and constituted by the American imaginary at a very early historical-cultural stage. Whitman articulates this very moment in "ur-form," precisely as a "potential within nature," unstoppable, and all about the future. He almost says it in as many words:

> Endless unfolding of words of ages!
> And mine a word of the modern, the word En-Masse.
> A word of the faith that never balks[19]

Sacvan Bercovitch has a particularly illuminating view of the potentiality of Whitman's poetry, one that fits well into the framework of the present discussion. Referring to D. H. Lawrence's complaints about the American poet's collapsing his self with the Eskimo, the squaw, and the slave, Bercovitch notes, "On one level, poetic specification here works as a rhetorical question to mask discrepancy," situated in historically circumscribed moments, and lingering in time "as a radical variation of symbolic identity. Whitman affirms the absolute, aesthetically, by particularizing it; and by particularizing it aesthetically, he invites us to question and challenge—and so potentially to decline or circumvent—the endgames of representative individualism."[20] It is precisely these invitations of possibilities that "Song of Myself" as variation entices in other aestheticizations of self and symbolic identity; for now, however, it must be remarked that the singing of absolutes is not for everyone.

That the self-realization in secular time referred to by Taylor is not, in this case, at least partly grounded in "higher time," is questionable, because the premises of "Song of Myself" as utterance of the American social imaginary and its place in modernity do not depend exclusively on the secularity of the modern social imaginary generally in order to allow for the unabashed singing of self. They also rely heavily on something resembling a mythological understanding of what America is and should be, and this is located above and beyond the American social imaginary as a structuring, cultural glue for bounded, national space. The powerful attraction of Whitman's writing lies in the template he crafted for and out of an enduring and complex institution that sustains and nourishes the perpetuation of the American imaginary at its deepest level. This is what I suggest constitutes a master imaginary, a culturological meta-understanding that resides in symbolism and myth and underlies the perpetuation of practices and understandings of the political and social everyday. The mythological element coincides with the aforementioned faith in the idea of the American project, a sensibility that already moves into the realm of the religious and the symbolic. It is a kind of creation story that, because it is carried forward through fundamental and in some senses universal human desires for progress, extends into perpetuity. The kind of mythical quality embedded in it certainly belongs to what Taylor describes as "the story (or myth) of progress, one of the most important modes of narration in modernity."[21]

I add that myth, or symbolism, is also at work on a different level, which very powerfully nourishes the disposition to pursue unfettered aspiration (Latin *aspirare* "to breathe upon," "to seek to reach," from *ad-* "to" + *spirare* "to breathe") as not only individually but also socially beneficial. This is powerful stuff, and in the American imaginary the impulse is encouraged and given free reign, since, as Taylor observes, "independence is thus a social, and not just a personal, ideal. It was valued as a contribution to national well-being and greatness and was correspondingly admired and lauded."[22] In the American case, the new arrangement of agents in relation to the social whole is based on a shared commitment to this new project, a sacred-secular conviction not only in the justice of the project's position in the world but in its goodness and universal application. *Enchantment* seems an appropriate designation for the embeddedness of such individual participation as social participation, performing its work along lines that are similar to norms obtaining in sacred time. "Time" is not quite "out of mind," as in Taylor's vocabulary, but perhaps closer to the time of mythos. It seems to stem from a combination that Bercovitch calls the "Winthrop variation," which gravitates around, on the one hand, the New World's answerability to the old world within the sacred parameters of the experiment, and the futurizing and seemingly inexhaustible possibilities this carries and, on the other, the historically coinciding temporal and spatial circumscription of a new (secular) way of being in the world. Out of this mesh proceeds a peculiarly ambiguous version of enchantment. The ambiguity is in part refracted in Whitman's "Song of Myself" as mediation between the transcendence of absolutes and the specificities of boundaries of identity that cannot be transgressed, between simultaneous exclusion and inclusion. The piece echoes a sacred-secular framework that is on a par with any archaic structural grid and that is resilient to questioning from the outside. The Latin *incantare*, meaning "to sing upon or against," is akin to the root of the word "enchantment," and "Song of Myself" may be heard as a chanting through the full register of the imaginary's range. Of course, when reading it alongside the "song" of a differently originated and originating imaginary that is borne forth from different routes, limitations also reveal themselves, and slightly different melodies are heard.

Song of Different Selves

In 1967 the Denver-born Chicano civil rights and political activist (and boxing champion) Rodolfo "Corky" Gonzales published his epic "I am Joaquín/Yo soy Joaquín." The visual layout of this work, with the English and Spanish versions facing each other, already hinted at the different nature of this other kind of self. The poem delineates roughly five centuries of historical routes that lead up to the moment of the enunciation and actualization of the persona of Joaquín in the United States of the 1960s. The register of names, events, and places is reminiscent of Whitman's catalogues, but with a crucial difference. Whereas Whitman's verbal constructions rarely depart from the present, future, or subjunctive tenses, audaciously looking ahead, Gonzales's lines are dominated by the past, past perfect, and present. This is not the most immediately noticeable difference: the retrospective gaze identifies a multitude of nodes that are all synecdochic representations of Mexican, American, and Mexican-American history and cultural traditions, each epitomizing different intersections and webs that reach into a maze of different directions and temporalities, as well as versions of America itself that are different from those found in Whitman's song.

The divergence of the temporal circumscriptions in "Song of Myself" and "I am Joaquín" is further accentuated by Gonzales's crisscrossing of sociohistorical and cultural paths without purporting to impose uniformity on them. This is a feature that "I am Joaquín" shares with a number of literary representations striving to locate a narrative and culturological space within the context of a larger, imposed one. On one level, one could include Whitman here. Surely, when writing America the Poem, he was doing exactly this, scripting into existence the shape of culturological nationhood. However, crucial differences remain. Whitman wrote for the future on a more or less blank slate. By contrast, Gonzales's epic has to be appreciated, not only against the backdrop of a particularly Mexican-American complex and the cultural and aesthetic *florecimiento* ("blossoming") that took place in tandem with the rise of the political Chicano movement in the 1960s and 1970s, but also against the much larger backdrop of global processes of colonization and their aftermaths involving a broader understanding of "America." As a narration of the cultural nation, "I am Joaquín" thus seeks the company of other far away songs such as the Ugandan poet Okot p'Bitek's "Song of Ocol" and "Song of Lawino," from 1966; Caribbean poet Derek Walcott's "Omeros"; and Pablo Neruda's "Canto General" (although this last is a slightly different case), to mention only a few. Even if Chicano literature does not originate in the same classical circumstances of colonization and decolonization as, for instance, African and West Indian literatures do, it has from its very beginning been infused with the urgent demands and strivings of representation and negotiation of culture and identity that generally characterize postcolonial literatures. Some historical background may be needed for readers who are not acquainted with this part of American history, so I briefly review how Mexican America came to be.

A little more than two decades after winning a hard-fought struggle for independence from Spain in 1821, Mexico lost half its territory to an ambitious newcomer to the north. The United States, a product of England's colonization of the New World, was driven by an unflinching conviction of its Manifest Destiny to rule from sea to shining sea, and, not entirely surprisingly, considered northern Mexico insufficiently populated and poorly enough "handled" to merit invasion and annexation. In Whitman's editorials in support of the war, he saw no reason why Mexico should not have to yield to his nation's progress. Most of his countrymen at the time felt the same. Including Texas, which had already been lost and after a short stint as the Lone Star republic joined the United States in 1845, Mexico lost half its territory. Mexican citizens became American citizens overnight and found themselves "an ethnic minority in a conquered land," or, as it has been more frequently suggested, internally colonized.[23] Until the 1960s and the rise of the civil rights movements, the Mexican-American minority existed in a kind of void, invisible, unaccounted for. This changed once and for all with the emergence of the Chicano movement and the artistic flowering that brought a whole army of writers and poets to attention, among them Gonzales. The first lines of "I am Joaquín" read as follows, and I quote them at length:

> I am Joaquín
> lost in a world of confusion,
> caught up in a whirl of a
> gringo society
> confused by the rules,
> scorned by attitudes,
> suppressed by manipulation,
> and destroyed by modern society.
> My fathers

have lost the economic battle
and won
The struggle of cultural survival.
And now!
I must choose
between
the paradox of
victory of the spirit,
despite physical hunger,
or
to exist in the grasp
of American social neurosis,
sterilization of the soul
and a full stomach.[24]

These lines introduce a persona and situate that persona at a preliminary point of departure, a site of enunciation from which routes and roots can be excavated, recorded, and restored. The words "between" and "or" are significantly singled out to stand alone, as visual reminders of the undetermined space from which the enunciation is launched. How very different are the premises for Joaquín's singing of self from those of Whitman: a sequence of forbidding designations—"lost," "caught up," "confused," "scorned"—hammers out a selfhood defined negatively, ending in a choice that essentially repeats the dichotomy of (transcendental) materialism versus idealism but is grounded in economic and social realities that the American imaginary rarely acknowledges.

Before a choice is made, however, the persona sings stories of glory and defeat, of pride and shame, of the one and the many that together form the totality of the trails leading up to the present moment: "I stand here looking back, / and now I see / the present / and still / I am the campesino / I am the fat political coyote / I / of the same name / Joaquín."[25] In contrast, Whitman's self carries no such baggage and can (again, in that imaginary's freedom from all constraints) depart from an uninhibited site of enunciation: "Born here of parents born here from parents the same, / and their parents the same, / I, now thirty-seven years old in perfect health begin, /

Hoping to cease not till death."[26] Right here is one of the more grave contrasts between the songs: "born here from parents the same" rings hollow in the context of Joaquín's loss of land and of routes in the American Southwest reaching back centuries before Whitman's moment.

The name "Joaquín" itself evokes several associations. To many readers, the legendary Mexican gold miner Joaquín Murieta immediately comes to mind. According to folklore he was a "peaceful Mexican miner whose claim was jumped by gold-greedy Anglos, who whipped him, hanged his brother, and raped his wife in his presence."[27] Murieta swore revenge, and in the narratives and songs that flourished in the mid-nineteenth century, he rose to a stature similar to that of Robin Hood. *The Robin Hood of El Dorado*, Walter Noble Burns's book from 1932, was indeed devoted to Murieta's story. Some readers may recall that Joaquín Murieta also figures as Zorro's younger brother in *The Mask of Zorro* (1998), a minor character to those not aware of the name and figure's semantic depths.

But "Joaquín" perhaps more meaningfully designates what Juan Bruce-Novoa calls a kind of "Chicano Everyman," not particularly better or worse than most.[28] This is underscored throughout the poem by the persona's arduous passage through the strata of history, as he identifies with high as well as low, poor as well as rich, white as well as brown. Joaquín traces the histories and trails constituting his complex self, starting with Cuauhtémoc of the Aztecs, "Proud and Noble/leader of men"; Nezahualcoyotl of the Acolhua, "Great leader of the Chichimecas"; and Cortés, "the despot"—admitting in the same breath that "I owned the land as far as the eye / could see under the crown of Spain, / and I gave my Indian sweat and blood / for the Spanish master / . . . I was both tyrant and slave."[29] The complex interlacing of heritages is repeated throughout, vacillating between heroes and villains, male and female, young and old:

I have been the bloody revolution,
The victor,
The vanquished,

I have killed
    and been killed.
            I am despots Díaz
            and Huerta
and the apostle of democracy,
            Francisco Madero.
I am
the black-shawled
faithful women
who die with me
or live
depending on the time and place.
I am
    faithful
        humble
            Juan Diego
            the Virgin of Guadalupe
            Tonantzin, Aztec Goddess too.[30]

This catalogue of types and of real events and persons may seem to echo Whitman exactly, but here we come to what is perhaps the most harrowing difference between the two works, to "I am Joaquín" as an utterance that profoundly locates itself on the outside of the grids of the master imaginary. The manner in which it does so can be related to human geographer Doreen Massey's suggestion of how to conceptualize space, namely as always under construction, as the product of interrelations and of co-constitutive multiplicities, "as a simultaneity of stories so-far."[31] As the passages from "I am Joaquín" reflect, the poem is both constituted by and constitutive of a space of precisely such "stories-so-far," which are brought into the persona's narrative as synecdochic references. They point to fragments of different historical spaces and trails and are brought under the simultaneity of the poetic utterance, but not in a single temporality. Whereas Whitman creates the "En-Masse" out of multiple trails (not always his own), which are subsumed into the present and a forward-gazing perspective that is unhampered and undeterred, Gonzales crafts what may be described as a heterochronistic moment, a space of momentousness that does not forget and whose exclusion from the central tenets of the imaginary, along with its own "routedness" in other kinds of "social-historical doing," forces the coexistence of multiple stories within his cultural moment of remembering. It poignantly allegorizes a wider context, as Mieke Bal has observed: "Migration is the situation of our time. But it is also an experience of time; as multiple, heterogeneous. The time of haste and waiting, the time of movement and stagnation; the time of memory and of an unsettling, provisional present, with its pleasures and its violence." In Bal's discussion, heterochronism takes on a deeper meaning, namely as the *experience* of multitemporality, and it carries momentous, narrative weight: "[heterochrony] disrupts the traditional linear narratives onto which routine responses and images are grafted, it offers temporal shelter to memories."[32] Throughout the multiple listings of culturological nodes of identification and routes, "Joaquín" engages heterochrony as a strategy of redemption through retrieval. In so doing, Gonzales writes a history of the American Southwest that, when it was first published, was rarely heard or recognized as having any legitimacy in a predominantly westward-looking historical and narrative imagination in which time is homogeneous, a single movement spreading over the continent in one direction only.

The contrasts between the two songs of different selves are everywhere at odds, in tension with each other, vying for representation. Discord is, however, perhaps nowhere more evident than in the evocation of the one work by the other in these few lines toward the end of "I am Joaquín":

> whatever I call myself,
> I look the same
> I feel the same
> I cry
> and
> sing the same.[33]

In these words reverberate the echo of the very first lines of "Song of Myself":

I celebrate myself, and sing myself,
And what I assume you shall assume,
For every atom belonging to me as good belongs to you.[34]

By superimposing "I cry and sing the same" onto "I celebrate myself," Gonzales shifts Whitman's song from unbridled optimism and all-embracing, future-oriented energy to a response that gazes backward and points toward the future with both reproach and defiance. The dialogue sets up "cry" against "celebrate," and the singing of a coherent self as metaphor for nation is countered with a self constituted along the principles of metonymic stubbornness that defies the kind of transference metaphor allows. It is the will to reconcile and persevere with and in conflict and difference, rather than the confidence in its resolution and dissolution, that propels Gonzales's song of self.

Moreover, Gonzales's overwriting here echoes another well-known response to Whitman, namely Langston Hughes's far more explicitly intertextual poem "I, Too," from 1925. From a perspective constituted by other and different routes within the American imaginary, Hughes's poem begins:

I, too, sing America
I am the darker brother.
They send me to eat in the kitchen
When company comes,
But I laugh,
And eat well,
And grow strong.[35]

Hughes here responds to Whitman's "I Hear America Singing" from 1860, rather than to "Song of Myself," but the self that the response addresses is not essentially different. In that poem, too, Whitman offers an inclusive metaphor of national coherence that Hughes then undermines by delineating exclusion and incoherence in its stead. However, while the persona points toward a future when he shall be on equal terms, Hughes does not leave the canvas of the Whitmanesque democracy that he engages. The axis of advancement and hence the expectation of progress according to the premises of the master imaginary are not fundamentally questioned. Again, Gonzales lays out a different route and forces his way out from underneath the imaginary's mantle: "I am Aztec Prince and Christian Christ / I SHALL ENDURE! / I WILL ENDURE!"[36] Rather than accepting the validity of Whitman's story-so-far as a point of orientation to be pursued, Gonzales locates alternative routes and alternative stories on whose rationale his persona proceeds to project different stories and different understandings of progress.

The main challenge to the master imaginary in Whitman's song thus resides in Joaquín's adamant insistence on the effect and perseverance of past routes and roots and on a framework anchored in the heterochronistic experience of contemporary cultural space. This challenge is also forcefully carried out in the generic framework itself. Whitman wrote in a free verse form that would carry the unique American experiment, a democracy of "counterpart of on the same terms," a form that could adequately reflect his enunciation of the imaginary, the "Endless unfolding of words of ages! / And mine a word of the modern, the word En-Masse."[37] Gonzales's poem follows in this nonmetrical and all-inclusive tradition, for "I am Joaquín" is first and foremost an American poem, insisting on its place in the American experience. As with the designation "Hispanic," the term "Chicano," meaning the politicized flank of the Mexican-American community, does not exist outside the United States: both coinages are native to American soil. This is not, however, the only reason why "I am Joaquín" is an American poem. A perhaps more profound reason is that the combination of influences that carries this text as a poem is inconceivable outside the culturological complex of the American Southwest.

In order to refract its American experience, "I am Joaquín" not only builds on the Whitmanesque catalogue and free verse but also draws heavily on a very different tradition of very different origins, namely the *corrido*, which is also native to the land and contemporary with Whitman's poetry. The heroic border *corrido* crystallized as a genre out of a particular set of sociopolitical circumstances and represented a revision of the already existing ballad tradition in greater Mexico. This form was related to the Spanish romance ballad, brought to New Spain with the conquistadores, continued in a somewhat scattered fashion in Mexico, and then surfacing as a dominant form of oral narrative in the latter half of the nineteenth century in what are today the Mexican-American border areas. According to José Limón's authoritative work on the history of the genre, the border *corrido*'s main revisions of the romance ballad can be summarized as follows: It moves from a nonstrophic, metrically diverse origin to strophic, metrically regular, complex rhyme schemes; it moves from serious and restrained to overflowing, as though, as Limón notes, "its wider melodic range were musically equipping the corrido to respond to a socially energetic moment." The narrator shifts from a detached, silent position delineating a dialogue between two principals to the first or third person, acting as witness to the events described, as a kind of news source.[38]

Thematically, we should note, the form shifts from celebrating fiestas, love affairs, and tournaments to celebrating the heroic deed, with an emphasis on male confrontations, until the core theme hardens, and, as the common definition goes, the border *corrido* comes to place "a common, peaceful workingman into an uncommon situation by the power of cultural and historical forces beyond his control. . . . In the process of this attempt to win social justice, his concern for his own personal life and his solitary fate must be put aside for the good of the collective life of his social group."[39] The hero's struggle invariably takes place, as the title of Américo Paredes's seminal work declares, "With His Pistol in His Hand."[40]

The border *corrido* therefore approximates folklore in terms of its typical themes and modes of dissemination. We tend to think of oral traditions as vehicles for expressing a given cultural group's shared way of life. As Richard Bauman puts it in his Introduction to Paredes's other important work, *Folklore and Culture on the Texas-Mexican Border*, the scholarly emphasis falls on "the role of folklore in sustaining group equilibrium and the maintenance of the social system." Bauman further emphasizes the important rerouting that Américo Paredes brought to this tradition and proposes a revisionist emphasis: "Certain elements of the Texas-Mexican repertoire (in folklore) . . . are part of the shared traditions of Greater Mexico, but this is only half the picture, for a significant portion of the repertoire, the most distinctive portion, is generated by the stark social oppositions of the border region, a response to differential—*not* shared—identity."[41] The relationship of Gonzales's poem to its generic ancestor is perhaps most evident on this latter point: "I am Joaquín" originates in and with conflict, a border strife where borders are multiple, and within which there are just as many identities and differences.

There is another way in which "I am Joaquín" draws on the *corrido* tradition, namely as a source of news. As noted earlier, if traditionally these were reports and stories from war or border struggles, the *corrido* has come to encompass almost anything that the singer and the audience consider newsworthy—and the realization of a Chicano cultural awareness and awakening would certainly count as news.[42] Consider also how Gonzales's poem was disseminated: only three months after its initial publication, "I am Joaquín" was picked up by Luis Valdez's traveling troupe *Teatro Campesino*, which created a collage of images, music, and voice-over readings of the poem that have been easy to present in communities.[43] The reproduction of "I am Joaquín" by means of mimeograph for cheap and effective distribution and readings in conferences and gatherings throughout the country adds to its function as a news source and witness. Finally, the thematic core that crystallized in the border *corrido* persists in "I am Joaquín," but instead of the traditional *corrido* hero, the narrator inserts himself in the story and then expands upon his own figure until the initial "I" has morphed into a collectivity of the multiple voices that the singer records and chronicles.

Joaquín's song draws on two coterminously emerging, generic ways of seeing the world, and they combine to carry this song of a different self. If social imaginaries trust the chronicles of cultural selfhood as a vehicle to instruct their participants as enabled members, then we should bear in mind that those very chronicles also organize themselves according to appropriate expectations and forms. Literary genres provide certain molds for refracting cultures' institutions and imaginaries, casts to shape their stories for the future. Bakhtin even argues that genres "are of a special significance," observing that "Genres (of literature and speech) throughout the centuries of their life accumulate ways of seeing and interpreting particular aspects of the world. For the writer-craftsman the genre serves as an external template, but the great artist awakens the semantic possibilities that lie within it."[44] Just as the imaginary as enabling filter is sustained by enabled practice, genres are sustained by their constant visitations and performances. In the case of "I am Joaquín," the particular combination of templates is a revisitation of its constitutive components, which in their traces replicate the fundamental ideas that on an ideological and epistemological level inform it, namely the necessary but uneasy amalgamations of individually and communally based outlooks. Observing how genres do their work is helpful for comprehending these confluences and their effects. As Hayden White observes:

> Cultural and social genres belong to culture and not to nature. . . . cultural genres do not represent genetically related classes of phenomena. . . . they are constructed for identifiable reasons and to serve specific purposes, and . . . genre systems can be used for destructive as well as for constructive purposes. So, genre is both "unnatural" and dangerous.[45]

None of this is to say, however, that distinctions between reasons and purposes in the case of Whitman and Gonzales can be neatly outlined, nor is this the primary concern here. Of greater relevance is the fact that (to modify my earlier distinction between underlying individually and communally based grids) *both* "I am Joaquín" and "Song of Myself" draw on the communal, but in wildly different ways. The *corrido* tradition demands the communally circumscribed and sanctioned hero, whereas Whitman's free verse assumes that role on the poet's own premises.[46] Consequently, in the generic amalgamation of "I am Joaquín," there occurs a combination of the two modes of enunciation, which appropriately reflects the in-between status of the Mexican-American tradition and community. A fusion of Whitman's ur-American free verse with the traditional border *corrido* thus materializes as a wholly new event in order to carry a different kind of imaginary, as the following lines make evident:

> Yes,
> I have come a long way to nowhere,

Unwillingly dragged by that
monstrous, technical
industrial giant called
Progress
and Anglo success . . .
I look at myself.
I watch my brothers.
I shed tears of sorrow.
I sow seeds of hate.
I withdraw to the safety within the
Circle of life—
MY OWN PEOPLE[47]

Gruesz's suggestion about Walt Whitman's writing, that it tends "to spatialize history and temporalize space," is no less true of Gonzales's work, but because the former tends toward a uniform moment of One, the spatial and temporal orientations in the two songs take rather different forms. Whitman's singing of self and nation runs along an axis of accommodation whereby difference is in *principle* erased (Whitman "is" the slave, he "is" the Indian, and so forth). In Gonzales's work, the relationships of the parts to the whole establish difference as the point of orientation. One could suggest that this is also the main point of contention between the two songs and their refractions of and relations to the American imaginary. Whitman sings the enchantment, he scripts the idealized as it should be, not as it is, hammering down the pillars of the imaginary in mythological time. "I am Joaquín" cannot perform like this, its reference points lie elsewhere, beyond myth and excluded from myth by history. This leads to a final observation regarding the function of these two songs in the context of bounded space as it coexists with the extended attraction of promise and advancement. The rendering, epic or otherwise, of a group's cultural or national space, tends to emphasize the proud lineage of one story only, a claim to a certain heritage and hence to a right of uncontested presence. On its deepest level this emotion informs what Orm Øverland, in his *Immigrant Minds, American Identities*, terms the creation of "homemaking myths," a strategy of storytelling that for a given ethnic group justifies, in his analyses, the United States as its "natural" home. Such myths, Øverland writes, are

> closely related to the kind of amateurish history writing that has been called "filiopietistic" because it invariably tells of the past excellence or greatness of a particular nation. . . . They have been the vehicles for a vision of an imagined America where a privileged immigrant group had an exclusive right to belong. . . . Each group created the stories anew and based them on myths and traditions of the old home country or on the real or imagined group experience in the new one.[48]

In Øverland's discussion, the American ethnic groups that figure in illustrations of such mythologized homes are mostly European: "[In] many foundation stories the history of the United States begins with the first arrival in the western hemisphere of a German, a Scandinavian, a Greek, a Jew or the 'representative' of some other nineteenth-century immigrant group."[49] "I am Joaquín" differs from these accounts in at least two critical ways. First, if homemaking myths tend toward the unidirectional and the monologic, and circumscribe place so that it is what Doreen Massey calls "closed, coherent, integrated as authentic; as 'home', a secure retreat; of space as somehow originarily regionalized, as always-already divided up," then "I am Joaquín" fulfils the homemaking function rather poorly. Instead of creating a proud lineage of one narrative, which would accomplish what Massey calls the "attempt to stabilize the meaning of particular envelopes of space-time,"[50] "I am Joaquín" admits and presents the full, and at times shameful and painful, register of trails:

> I look at myself
> And see part of me
> Who rejects my father and my mother
> And dissolves into the melting pot
> To disappear in shame.[51]

In contrast, for all its multifarious, all-encompassing, and diverse addresses and the trails it stakes out, "Song of Myself" resounds convincingly and precisely as a strategy of homemaking, and this is ultimately a structural rather than thematic accomplishment. The poetics of the temporal and the spatial become one, and the expanding moment underscores the legitimacy and authenticity of its simultaneous claim to place. The song frames and institutes the imaginary's (inherently future-oriented) promise safely within the myth of progress.

This is not to say that "I am Joaquín" lays no claim to the space it occupies, narratively or culturally. The space of the Mexican-American is, however, densely sedimented, a palimpsest of overwritings and erasures within Massey's "always-already divided up." The oldest layer of known human history in the present context is of course the Native American and the native Mexican, preceding all other presences by centuries. More recently, but still long before Anglos settled in the West, while the American Southwest was still New Spain and later northeastern Mexico, the land was crisscrossed with Spanish place-names in a web of roads, towns, and missions. Out of this complexity a different conceptualization of space necessarily follows. If, according to Sacvan Bercovitch's previously cited argument, Whitman, in his aesthetic particularizing of the absolute, invites us to question and challenge the endgames of representative individualism, then "I am Joaquín's" invitation extends farther, to challenge the endgame of representative "culturalism." Gonzales's particularization of those points on the culturological itinerary that he delineates at the very outset serves to destabilize all notions of absolutes and instead carves out a rejoinder to the imaginary of Whitman's song by speaking compellingly to the imagination of space as the product of interrelations in continuous flux. Myth and idealism suffuse both poems, but Gonzales's song charts trails that, as Massey reminds us, mark how "the spatial is social relations stretched out. The fact is . . . that social relations are never still; they are inherently dynamic."[52] They are indeed, and there is something deeply ironic about the situation of the imaginary today: not only has the Mexican-American minority by some accounts spread over the original location of the mythical homeland of Aztlán, thereby rerouting the momentum that once propelled the United States' expansion from East to West, but that minority also includes descendants of the original inhabitants, Mesoamerican Indians who do not necessarily even speak Spanish, and they, too, announce their entry. I return to these movements and their implications in chapter 6, but first I turn to a very different response to and refraction of the American imaginary, in which the notion of institution takes a slightly different form.

[4]

THE "LONG EMPTY MOMENT": RICHARD FORD'S *THE SPORTSWRITER*

We live alone in our own core, flitting over the surface now and then, pretending.—Ana Menéndez, *In Cuba I Was a German Shepherd*

IN CHARLES TAYLOR'S EXPOSITION, one of the main characteristics of the modern social imaginary is its severance from significations and practices grounded in religious time or origins, what he calls a "time out of mind." He remarks that "Modernity is secular, not in the frequent, rather loose sense of the word, where it designates the absence of religion, but rather in the fact that religion occupies a different place, compatible with the sense that all social action takes place in profane time."[1] But this does not mean the utter absence of alternative constructs that embed, of the emergence of other symbolic spheres, alternative mythological anchorages that are as persuasive and total as the inherently sacred paradigms of archaic times. In the end, the drive of mobility from station to station in life, personal and collective, hinges on the participants' conviction of the righteousness of the actualization of these ideals, and in the final instance, the ideals are sacrosanct, as many a foreigner to the American imaginary has discovered. It is precisely the confidence in the inherent good of the project that comes to constitute this imaginary as enabling and enabled filter, a curious veil that is most profane, yet simultaneously sacred and therefore ever renewable, even portable. It is indeed the case that religion in our day "occupies a different place, compatible with the sense that all social action takes place in profane time," but one wonders, in the case of the American manifestation of modernity, whether this means that social action and the myth of progress are collapsed into a modality best characterized as sacred-secular. In that case, attaining a "clean" perspective is nearly impossible: wherever you are, there you are, and you are invariably a fragment of the imaginary to which you belong. It follows that it becomes as unimaginable to step outside this mythological-social parameter as it was in Castoriadis's example referred to in chapter 1: "A Hindu of the past who would decide to ignore the existence of the castes, would most likely be mad—or would soon become so."[2] Such a decision rejects the very premises on which that imaginary is founded, and with them the belief and willingness to participate in its practices and institutions. This is neither plausible nor desirable.

And yet it may have been Bartleby, Herman Melville's notorious scrivener and Walt Whitman's contemporary, who first voiced such a mad rejection of the American imaginary, a flat-out refusal to take part. "I prefer not to" resounds across the decades, bemusing generation upon generation of students and scholars of American literature. The question of what Melville's obscure character prefers not to do, or not to be, is among the obligatory riddles found on many a college reading list, commonly illustrating the skeptical currents in early American literary and intellectual culture. Read as a response to and from the reach of the American imaginary, however, the tenor of Bartleby's stubborn reiteration has a more radical sound. As a "mad" rejection of participation itself, it is an outright repudiation of the core of the project. Indeed, it stands as a negation of the faith in the validity of individually and communally held ideals of transference and progress that both uphold the imaginary and are upheld by it in turn. "I prefer not to" relegates the obstinate scrivener to a place firmly on the outside of the American imaginary, and the negation of the faith-driven ideas of metamorphosis and transformation, of boundless mobility and progress, must result in the immobilization that in the end annihilates Bartleby.

Such madness of utter refusal is not the rule, but when confronted with the mythology of perpetual progress, we do find in American literature a tradition that configures social and individual torpor. A powerful strand speaks of and to alienation and apathetic withdrawal from the demands and expectations of the imaginary, searching for the proper outlet, the right addressee for an unease that is not always clearly identifiable. I now proceed to explore the configuration of this particular kind of response in Richard Ford's acclaimed novel *The Sportswriter*. In a manner similar to Melville's reduction of Bartleby's refusal to partake into the brief "I prefer not to," thereby configuring his existence into utter immobility and finally death, Ford follows and scripts his sportswriter on a sliding scale of static apathy. Moreover, his portrayal of the alienated subject in the midst of postmodern life gives existential crisis a current form, on the foremost contemporary stage at the very heart of the American imaginary, the suburb. The relationship between suburban aesthetics and the protagonist of *The Sportswriter* is impossible to ignore, and perhaps the most poignant attributions are the tropological spillovers from a particular version of this space into a narrative mode of hazy monotony and semi-apathy, even indifference, which extends to and lies over character description, structure, and thematic exposition. The upshot is a conflation of the boundaries between the main character's epistemological senses of interiority and exteriority into a lethargic sameness, echoing Bartleby's immobility as a stark response to the ideas and ideals of the life deemed desirable by most.

"My name is Frank Bascombe. I am a sportswriter."[3] With these words, the protagonist and narrator begins his story. In the course of an Easter weekend, Frank will meet his ex-wife at the grave of their oldest son, as he does every year; fly out to Detroit with his new girlfriend Vicki Arcenault to do an interview with a disabled football player for a human-interest story; identify the corpse of a fellow member of the Divorced Men's Club; break up with Vicki; leave for France with a girl twenty years his junior; and end up in Florida to stay with relatives he has never met. To some readers, the opening phrase will resonate with another famous introduction: "Call me Ishmael." Like Melville's narrator in *Moby Dick*, Frank displays the characteristics of an ancient biblical figure, the outcast and lonely survivor. But while the biblical Ishmael emerged from the desert to come into a literal as well as metaphorical presence, and while Melville's Ishmael ascends from the ocean to create his narrative, Frank's surfacing is more diffuse. The uncertainty originates in the text's marked resistance to positing the boundaries that figuration typically relies on, and in its allowing the absence of distance to become the main trope itself. This abstract quality replicates the setting of the narrative, and even if *The Sportswriter* is not, strictly speaking, a novel of the suburb, the institution of the suburb, its aesthetics, and its ideology are nevertheless crucial to the generation of forms and figures in Frank's apathetic response to the imaginary that embeds him.

Frank's story unfolds in Haddam, New Jersey, a suburb whose insistent neutrality and resistance to interruptions and breaches enhance his growing sense of alienation. The significance of suburbia as the stage set for *The Sportswriter* makes some consideration of the suburb in its American cultural and literary context of imaginary ideal necessary to appreciate its refraction in the novel's tropological grammar. To do this, I refer to the suburban as it permeates a certain strand of literature and film, and to its function as an affirmative space of relief from cultural contestations in the broader sense. One of the most poignant contributions of *The Sportswriter* is the quiet, aestheticized acceptance of the protagonist's resignation in the face of his obligation to perpetuate and uphold faith. This novel does not defy the premises of the imaginary, nor does the text battle against its sway. Indeed, the novel reads in a broader perspective thematically than what I am focusing on here. Ford's representation of inertia, set psychologically against the concreteness of a particular kind of habitat, does, however, invite a reading of the text as participating in a conversation moving from and to the demands and expectations of the American imaginary.

The concreteness of *The Sportswriter*'s setting in Haddam is emblematic of the qualities and characteristics that in 1961 Lewis Mumford diagnosed and cautioned against, in an admonition that remains aesthetically, sociologically, and ideologically relevant. In an early assessment of the suburb, Mumford concluded that it is

> inhabited by people of the same class, the same income, the same age group, witnessing the same television performances, eating the same tasteless pre-fabricated foods, from the same freezers, conforming in

> every outward and inward respect to a common mold, manufactured in the central metropolis. Thus the ultimate effect of the suburban escape in our time is, ironically, a low-grade uniform environment from which escape is impossible.[4]

Even before this, the possibility or impossibility of escape that this passage describes had increasingly become a major focus in representations of the suburb, in literature as well as movies. Some critics claim that no great literature has emanated from this segment of American cultural life, as when Philip T. Nicholson laments, "Who sings the song of the suburbs? Where is the poet? Where is the Woody Guthrie of Woodmere, the Sinclair Lewis of Levittown? Some fine novelists have set their stories and characters in suburban communities, but the setting is typically a backdrop, a tableau, for a look at characters and stories whose meaning transcends their place."[5] This is, as others have pointed out, a somewhat misguided perspective. Robert Beuka, for instance, counters with the argument that: "Rather than being randomly or accidentally placed, [the suburban works under examination] are situated specifically and precisely in suburban communities that are themselves amalgams of various social and cultural anxieties—places that might be read, in geographer Yi-Fu Tuan's terminology, as 'landscapes of fear.'"[6] And it is true that, already in the 1920s with a writer such as F. Scott Fitzgerald, but especially from the 1950s, the human limitations of the suburb have been problematized, gauged, despaired at. Sloan Wilson in *The Man in the Grey Flannel Suit*, Sinclair Lewis with his *Babbitt* trilogy, John Updike, John Cheever, Don DeLillo, Joyce Carol Oates, David Gates, Frederick Barthelme, and Jonathan Franzen are some names that mark the suburb's persistence as a focal point in a topography of alienation that profoundly destabilizes the desirability of one of the American imaginary's principal institutions. And there should be nothing unexpected about this; as Paul Knox observes, the suburb, its growth, and its development are "a consequence of modernity, an expression of modernity, and a conditioner of modernity."[7]

From its beginnings, the suburb offered and emphasized a safe retreat from city centers, a safe and private environment in which to raise children, a space neither rural nor urban, but something in between, or perhaps, as one of the insistent themes in films and fiction suggests, neither. It is in this sense an inherently liminal place, but not the kind filled with the potential creativity of the threshold, or Homi Bhabha's concept of third space as ethical possibility. It is a space that perhaps shares characteristics more closely with Michel Foucault's concept of *heterotopos*, a "counter-emplacement," real places that are "written into the institution of society itself," in which "all the other real emplacements that can be found within culture, are simultaneously represented, contested and inverted; a kind of places that are outside all places, even though they are actually localizable." I shall not discuss in detail the exact relationship between the six principles that Foucault lists as descriptive of heterotopos; it is the last one that is particularly relevant here. It has a compensatory function in relation to the rest of space, as "another real space, as perfect, as meticulous, as well arranged as ours is disorderly."[8] Consider this in relation to the following description of the early Levittown suburbs: "Everybody lives on the same side of the tracks. They have no slums to fret about, no families of conspicuous wealth to envy, no traditional upper crust to whet and thwart their social aspirations."[9] The newspaper pictures a scenario that almost exactly replicates the Foucauldian conception of "other space" as fulfilling a function of perfection outside of general, inhabited space, often resolving conflicts over race and class—ordering the messy and multicultural into a homogeneous picture. The sameness of the suburb, at least in earlier years (today, gated communities have tended to take over that role), encloses the suburban participant in a modified yet Jeffersonian independence, safely secured, as the previous quotation has it, for unhindered social aspiration.

This particular "other space" is supposed to fulfil a dream, and it marks the proper stage of proper progress, an enveloping of individual aspirations in a framed and curiously communal finished product. The suburb's promise is, ultimately, the promise of a self-reliance that configures original ideas of individual progress and pursuit belonging to an Arcadian or pioneer spirit into what Cornelius Castoriadis calls second-order institutions. He divides this category into two subcategories. The first is transhistorical, exemplified by institutions such as family and language: their exact organization varies according to period and place, but they are invariably present in some form in all societies and at all times. The other is the category of "second-order institutions specific to particular societies and playing an absolutely central role in them, in that these specific institutions are the essential embodiments of what is of vital importance to that societal institution, its social imaginary significations."[10] To this category, I suggest, belongs the suburb. And if we return to the idea of heterotopos as compensatory perfection, the line can be drawn rather effortlessly from Castoriadis's "essential embodiments" both to other space as the countersite that is "formed in the very founding of society," and to the suburb as enchanted in the sense of Knox's article cited earlier. The word does not connote quite the same thing as it does when Charles Taylor refers to the enchanted and the disenchanted; in the present context "enchanted" connotes one of the manifestations of magic, the spell, for better or for worse.

None of this is unique to America, but there the institution may have reached its perfect, most widespread, and most continuously adaptive form, which has not gone unnoticed. However, in the multiple representations of the suburb in movies and literature, especially in the last several decades, irony and sarcasm have tended to dominate the narrative mode. This creates a certain distance between the subject matter and the viewer, a breach. Since the subject matter in these representations tends to center on alienation and detachment, on emotional and aesthetic conflation, the breach goes some way toward sparing the reader or viewer the full impact of the message that these movies and texts at least sometimes attempt to convey. One example is Sam Mendes's *American Beauty* (1999), in which the protagonist's acute and deepening sense of slowly drowning in the demands of conformity and materialism brings him to a point of personal crisis that eventually leads to his death. However, shades of humorous and satirical metacommentary soften the relentlessness of the topic, and in the end the movie passes for an astute, funny observation, but not much more. Todd Solondz's roughly contemporary *Happiness* (1998) and *Welcome to the Doll-*

house (1995), on the other hand, refract a more nuanced probing into these pressures and characters' emotional responses. The destructive forces that at every moment threaten to erupt in the lives of the well-adjusted suburbanites underlie the narration and filmic composition in both movies, in such a way as never to slacken the tension between the demands for material conformity and the spirit that yearns for fulfilment and remains unrequited. The most powerful of these is, in my opinion, *Welcome to the Dollhouse*, whose ending leaves the adolescent protagonist alone with her dejected defeat after her attempt to break out, forcing a rupture in the detached evenness of her home. With tears streaming down her cheeks, she is thoroughly secured in her designated place, seated and surrounded by singing, well-adjusted kids in a school bus en route to summer camp.

As a last illustration, I highlight the part of Stephen Daldry's *The Hours* (2002) (the filmic representation that I think most resembles Ford's handling of alienation) that focuses on Laura Brown, one of three female protagonists, who is played by Julianne Moore. Laura's depressed aloofness is visualized for us through her surroundings and her interaction with them. Her movements around the house are slow; she moves among sterile and impersonal furniture. Even though her little son is near her all the time, he is never actually *with* her. We see him looking at his mother from over the back of a chair, from behind a corner, from over the kitchen counter—always from a distance. In one of the film's most poignant scenes, an eye-level shot shows the boy in the front seat of a car, looking at his mother driving, and behind him, through the car window, rows of identical houses slowly pass by. What the viewer sees is what the mother does not see, or what she cannot any longer bear to see. Her depression is thus masterfully figured before us as the conflation of the utmost intimacy of her son's beseeching glance on the inside, and the indifferent public display of anonymity on the outside, the engine's monotonous drone the only accompaniment to both.

It is this peculiar lack of discreetness, of distinctions and boundaries, that also characterizes Richard Ford's novel: no irony, no loophole, no dramatic turning point allows him—or the reader—to step outside the all-encompassing, isolated, and isolating drone. The monotony in *The Sportswriter* also extends to the narrative's representation of temporality. Consider for instance the following passage, in which Frank muses on the usability, as it were, of the past:

> My own history I think of as a postcard with changing scenes on one side but no particular or memorable messages on the back. You can get detached from your beginnings, as we all know, and not by any malevolent designs, just by life, fate, the tug of the ever-present. The stamp of our parents and of the past in general is, to my mind, overworked, since at some point we are whole and by ourselves upon the earth, and there is nothing that can change that for better or for worse, and so we might as well think about something more promising.[11]

This juxtaposition of oblivion and remembrance effectuates a temporal orientation that is all about and in the present. Consequently, the narrative voice rejects the existence of boundaries on a very fundamental level, for as Reinhold Görling succinctly puts it: "Borders have to do with traces, which can be understood as territorializations or as spatializations of time. A trace is a recorded difference and a sign of a difference; in other words, a juncture of movement and archive, or memory."[12] We could broaden this and suggest that borders and boundaries are the manifestations of time arrested; they are what succeed the breach and its figuration in the territorial divisions marking the end or the beginning of national or cultural space; in the instrument's spatializing of a phrase; in the visual impression of color grating against color, of form encountering form; in the immobility of the statue's straining in the midst of the mobility that it represents; in the sudden moment that eyes in the crowd meet. In one way or another, these are all stoppages of time, in which discreet spaces engage with each other, if only momentarily. The immobility of the statue is caught in a temporality that violently protests the flow of the present in the beholder's eye. The sudden sight of someone in a crowd is precisely this, a breach where flow and simultaneity as stillness collide: "The apparition of these faces in the crowd." In all of these instances, our perception and recognition hinge on temporal arrest, on breach. *The Sportswriter*, however, resists these arrests. To borrow a phrase from one of Frank's many solipsisms, his is the narrative of the "long empty moment."[13]

Having lived with his wife in New York for a while, Frank tells us, he one day decided it was time to get out of the city and move to a place where "I knew no one and no one knew me and I could perfect my important writer's anonymity." The choice fell on Haddam, New Jersey, "a plain, unprepossessing and unexpectant landscape." Throughout the book, the white, middle-class suburb of Haddam remains nondescript, neither pleasant nor unpleasant: "all in all it's not an interesting town to live in, but that's the way we like it."[14] The characterization resonates strongly with the founder, so to speak, of the literary trope of suburban alienation. Beuka suggests that Sinclair Lewis, more than anyone, scripted a representation of estrangement that has been worked and reworked ever since:

> By using the trappings of the suburban setting to indicate his protagonist's immersion in a banal world or convention and creature comforts—describing Babbitt's house, the narrator informs us that "Though there was nothing in [it] that was interesting, there was nothing that was offensive"—Lewis fashioned a trope that would be repeated in virtually all subsequent fiction.[15]

Beuka's words, as well as those of the narrator he cites, complement Frank and his assessment of his surroundings well. In *The Sportswriter* the landscape itself resists demarcations that break up its levelled and monotonous impression, forestalling any hint of breach and, certainly, any hint of irony. Similarly, when Frank remembers the time following his son's death, he recalls that both he and his wife (tellingly referred to simply as "X") spent hours going through mail-order catalogues. This bizarre therapeutic exercise is recounted matter-of-factly, conveying that the bereaved couple dreamed themselves into the safety of a world of comfortable objects and exterior perfection:

> X and I came to believe, for a time, that satisfying all our purchasing needs from catalogues was the very way of life that suited us and our circumstances; that we were the kind of people for whom catalogue-

> buying was better than going out into the world and wasting time in shopping-malls, or going to New York, or even going out into the shady business streets of Haddam to find what we needed.[16]

The reader learns why Frank became a sportswriter, that he abandoned a promising career as a novelist because he was unable to write a second novel. The reason, one reason among several but nevertheless the main one, was that he lost his sense of anticipation, "the sweet pain to know whatever's next—a must for a real writer."[17] Reflecting on his current profession as a sportswriter for a glossy sports magazine, Frank ponders:

> Why, you might ask, would a man give up a promising literary career—there were some good notices—to become a sportswriter?
>
> It's a good question. For now let me say only this: if sports writing teaches you anything, and there is much truth to it as well as plenty of lies, it is that for your life to be worth anything you must sooner or later face the possibility of terrible, searing regret. Though you must also manage to avoid it or your life will be ruined.
>
> I believe I have done these two things. Faced down regret. Avoided ruin. And I am still here to tell about it.[18]

I referred initially to the evocation of other survival narratives. Here too, as Fred Hobson has pointed out, we hear the echo of Job from the "Epilogue" to *Moby Dick*: "And I only am escaped alone to tell thee."[19] But unlike Ishmael, who was saved by Queequeg's coffin, Frank in his survival is, as Edward Dupuey has observed, closer to Walker Percy's ex-suicide, a "person for whom '*[t]o be or not to be* becomes a true choice, where before you were stuck with *to be*.'"[20] This condition is hinted at early on in *The Sportswriter*. Reflecting on his relationship to his ex-wife, Frank notes: "Toward the end of our marriage I got lost in some kind of dreaminess." The exact reason for and nature of this dreaminess is then left unexplored for a while, until, after a preliminary retreat into his past and the question of why he has ended up where he is, Frank explains dreaminess as "among other things, a state of suspended recognition, and a response to too much and useless factuality." While he admits that his condition may have something to do with the death of his oldest son, he does not think it explains everything: "I'm unwilling to say that that was the cause, or that anything is ever the sole cause of anything else. I know that you can dream your way through an otherwise fine life, and never wake up, which is what I almost did. I believe I have survived that now and nearly put the dreaminess behind me." When Frank describes his rather noncommittal membership in something informally called the Divorced Men's Club, the state of dreaminess assumes a slightly different character. Here Frank muses in more general terms that "We simply try to settle into our lost-ness as comfortably and with as much good manners and little curiosity as we can. And perhaps the only reason we have not quit is that we can't think of a compelling reason to. When we do think of a good reason we'll all no doubt quit in an instant. And I may be getting close."[21]

Against emptiness and nonconsequence, that is, against apathy, Frank and his narrative only give us more of the same, offering not resistance but instead a polite compliance with the "factualities" of existence. There are several ways of approaching this aspect of the text. Hobson, for instance, observes that

> Ford is indeed a discriminating writer, but he is also a writer who would object less to the excesses of popular culture than to a particular view—call it elitist or privileged—that would pass judgment on that culture. It is precisely this resistance to easy irony, a resistance to the *temptation* to be ironic in dealing with popular culture, that distinguishes Ford from numerous other contemporary writers; for if an ironic vision is generally assumed to be a literary virtue, such a transcendence of accessible irony—or, perhaps, a deeper irony that turns on itself, ironizing the ironists—may be even more desirable.[22]

Hobson succinctly locates the distinctive voice of Ford's work, but the implication is that irony is nevertheless involved, if not on the most readily accessible level. However, what if irony is simply not part of Frank Bascombe's worldview? What if, as in Bill Owens's peculiar book of snapshots *Suburbia*, where he documented his neighbors' lives in Livermore, California, the suburb and its aesthetic are simply portrayed as they are, from a position beyond elitist disdain or other objectifications, one in which the persons in the pictures have, as Owens matter-of-factly introduces his photos, "realized the American Dream. They are proud to be homeowners and to have achieved material success."[23] Does a similar absence of distance lessen the literary quality of *The Sportswriter*?

Or, as some critics have done, do we have to illuminate Ford's Frank Bascombe via other traditions and thereby provide the justification that we feel we need to explain this epistemological collapse? For instance, if we place Ford within the Southern tradition, will that clarify things? Hobson argues that Frank may be closer to the ur-Southern character Quentin Compson than Ford is willing to admit, and that the novel is firmly entrenched in the Southern literary tradition. Ford himself has expressed some exasperation with critics' desire to have him fit neatly into this camp, and for that reason he has set all his stories except the first two in specifically non-Southern places. Hobson suggests, however, with quite convincing references to *The Sportswriter*, that "the lady doth protest too much":

> Frank's great interest in the absence of past, of historical burden, of family heritage, of fixed place, of community suggests a southern mind that is fascinated by these things. A true disregard of place, of history, would require an unconsciousness of it, and Frank has anything but that. . . . It is Frank Bascombe—who resembles in many ways his creator—saying, "I'm not interested in the South. I'm not. I'm not."[24]

Hobson suggests that the disregard in Ford's Frank Bascombe novels for the significance (and burden) of place, tradition, and memories may in fact be homage per negation to the Southern tradition. Such a reading certainly sheds light on the Frank Bascombe character in unexpected and interesting ways, and adds an element to the Southern tradition itself that opens up intriguing vistas. For my purposes here, however, it is the discursive figuration of conflation, of the presence of absence and indifference, which ultimately forms something close to a Bartleby-esque rejection of the imaginary's enchantment, that provides the most rewarding pathway into this novel. For if, as in enchanted, embedding imaginaries of the past, taking a stance outside of the imaginary's reach is not an option, then indifference and refusal to partake perhaps are. Moreover, approaching *The Sportswriter* in this manner, as the narrative analogizes a whole subset of practices lived in second-order institutions, enables commentary on modernity's foremost disease, alienation, from a slightly different angle.

The process of figuration in Ford's literary craftsmanship crystallizes only gradually. For instance, after the death of his son, but before his marriage to X ends, Frank indulges in a series of nonsensical, short relationships and one-night stands, eighteen to be exact, all in order to enter into a different life. This is much like sifting through mail-order catalogues for the comfort of those glossy, safe lives: "What I was doing . . . was trying to be within myself by being as nearly as possible *within* somebody else. It is not a new approach to romance. And it doesn't work. In fact, it leads to a terrible dreaminess and the worst kind of abstractions and unreachableness."[25]

While this is told in retrospect, the trip to Detroit ("city of lost industrial dreams, floats out around us like a mirage of some sane and glaciated life"), and the interview with the disabled football player, take place in the present. That meeting turns out to be painfully meaningless when it becomes clear that Herb, the interview object, no longer has the ability to look at the future with any real sense of faith and so torpedoes Frank's human-interest story. As he leaves Herb, Frank reflects: "It is the sadness of elusive life glimpsed and unfairly lost, and the following, lifelong contest with bitter facts." Frank's response to this sadness is to invoke his mantra of avoiding what he has earlier called "searing regret": "Only I do not want to feel it and won't. It is too close to regret to play fast and loose with. And the only thing worse than terrible regret is unearned terrible regret."[26]

Other incidents could be pointed out: the dinner at Vicki's house, when Frank is introduced to the family and already knows that it is too little, too late; the several telephone conversations with X, all ending on an ever-deferring note of sadness and what is truly a state of dreaminess and "suspended recognition." The only time Frank comes close to being actually present in a human relationship, to engaging affectively, is in his new if hesitant friendship with a fellow member of the Divorced Men's Club. He is partly propelled into it by Walter's sudden confession to him that he has had sex with a perfect stranger, and a man at that. After what seems to Walter an intimate moment (which is the nature of any confession), he tries to forge a real friendship with Frank, but the latter is reluctant and avoids any further deepening of the relationship: "Don't call, my silent message says, I'll be sleeping. Dreaming sweet dreams. Don't call. Friendship is a lie of life. Don't call." When Walter eventually shoots himself, however, Frank is jolted into at least a semblance of affective presence, and he comes closer than before to articulating the gestalt of his dreaminess, now rephrased as invisibility: "Walter would say that I have become neither the seer nor the thing seen. . . . I drive, an invisible man, through the slumberous, hilled, post-Easter streets of Haddam. And as I have already sensed, it is not a good place for Death. Death's a preposterous intruder. A breach." Frank quickly reinstalls dreaminess as invisibility into his being-as-choice: "Haddam is, however, a first-class place for invisibility—it is practically made for it."[27]

And Frank goes on dreaming himself into invisibility, in France, with a young girl he meets in the Gotham offices of his sports magazine, after he flees Haddam. As the novel ends, Frank is hopeful: "And there is no nicer time on earth than now—everything in the offing, nothing gone wrong, all potential." He is, however, hopelessly lost in the "long empty moment" that has shown itself over and over again to paralyze him in abstraction and isolation, and, indeed, the main part of the novel ends with Frank's thinking: "No one's noticed me standing here at all."[28] It bears emphasizing, however, that the various representations of Frank's being-as-choice are identifiable neither to Frank nor to the reader until the "Epilogue." Until that point, the reader, as well as the narrator, is far too immersed in the monotonous and levelled narrative to be able to conceptualize this choice as an ideational position, a deliberate act on the part of the protagonist. Throughout the story the convergence of backdrop, plot, and character has been complete, indifference met with indifference. In the "Epilogue," however, Frank's perspective is different. A new sensibility to and engagement with temporality is noticeable:

> I am usually (if only momentarily) glad to have a past, even an imputed and remote one. There is something to that. It is not a burden, though I've always thought of it as one. I cannot say that we

> all need a past in full literary sense, or that one is much useful in the end. But a small one doesn't hurt, especially if you're already in a life of your own choosing.[29]

When we consider that Frank has previously discarded the usability of the past, this reflection marks a definite turning point. More importantly, his mere acknowledgment of the existence of a past recognizes the existence of a temporal boundary and allows for an interruption in the narrative's even flow. "Dreaminess" expands and mutates slightly, into "lost-ness," all but vanishes again as "invisibility," and then becomes more distinct again as a "film": "And I thought that one natural effect of life is to cover you in a thick layer of . . . what? A film? A residue or skin of all the things you've done and been and said and erred at? I'm not sure."[30] Frank's one-dimensional narrative is a vehicle for his focus on maintaining the emotional and intellectual balance of avoiding "searing regret" while still "remaining human." This project is conceivable only through the absence of a breach. There must be no distinction marking the inside of Frank's existence as apart from or contradicting the outside; this would generate a boundary from which regret almost certainly would be configured. In the breach of Frank's acknowledgment of a past (even though a "small" one), however, a figure with a distinguishable tenor appears, and paradoxically, it is absence, framing the "long empty moment."

The tropological mode in which this configuration comes about belongs to metonymy. As David Lodge observes of the opening paragraph in *A Passage to India*, "It is metonymic writing, not metaphoric, even though it contains a few metaphors and no metonymies; it is metonymic in structure, connecting topics on the basis of contiguity, not similarity."[31] So too in *The Sportswriter*. Whereas metaphor leaps and jumps across discreet conceptual spaces, forging new connections and constellations out of dissimilar spheres that provide outlets of differentiation, metonymy is confined by the principle of contiguity. The varied representations of the same, in this case the apathy of the "long empty moment," are carried out according to this basic principle. In the end, as we have seen, the description is taken to an extreme through the ultimate positing of a property that is closely associated with the whole as *identical* to the whole. Constituted by and constitutive of absence, of nonbreach, Frank must remain within the confines of contiguity, of "same-ness." Transgression would mean breach, and a breach would imply the overwhelming likelihood of a figuration, which the character's objective of remaining unaffected could not sustain.

The Sportswriter, therefore, can be read as an arrangement of loneliness and alienation. The process that generates it, however, originates at a point prior to the actual tropological manifestation, marking what Mikhail Bakhtin refers to as the architectonics of meaning as follows: "the intuitionally necessary, non-fortuitous disposition and integration of concrete, unique parts and moments into a consummated whole can exist only around a given human being as a hero."[32] Frank's tale of nothingness and its despair, surging from nothingness and its gloom, is ordered around him in an architectonic order, in which a multitude of parts and moments all strive to break away from Lacan's "rails of metonymy, eternally extending toward the *desire for something else*."[33] Frank is only able to escape these rails when he gets a glimpse of a life not covered by the "film," from a conceptual space that is not implicated in and by them. If only momentarily, situating himself outside the simultaneity of his empty moment allows the figure to emerge and speak:

> But you are under it [the film], and for a long time, and only rarely do you know it, except that for some unexpected reason or opportunity you come out—for an hour or even for a moment—and you suddenly feel pretty good. . . . Have you been ill, you ask. Is life itself an illness or a syndrome? Who knows?[34]

"The relation of the Figure to its isolating place defines a 'fact': 'the fact is . . . ,' 'what takes place is . . . ' Thus isolated, the Figure becomes an Image, an Icon." Gilles Deleuze's introductory comments in his work on Francis Bacon's paintings bear on the process of figuration in *The Sportswriter*. In fact, there is a remarkable resemblance between Ford's subtle handling of isolation and alienation and the representation of isolated horror in some of Francis Bacon's paintings. The relationship in Bacon's art between the recurring oval shape and the human shape placed on it or inside it is what creates the "straining figure" in all its immobile and lonely fright. Since the contours of the human figure are often distorted and diffuse, and, more importantly, are painted onto or even as part of the frame against which they are contrasted, it takes us a while to discern these contours of the emerging figure. As Deleuze observes, it is in their relationship to the oval shape or field that people in Bacon's paintings form a figure. He compares the field to a circus ring, "a kind of amphitheatre as 'place.'" The "place" may also be a round area, a cube, bars, but the important thing, Deleuze argues, is that "they do not consign the Figure to immobility but, on the contrary, render sensible a kind of progression, and exploration of the Figure within the place, or upon itself. It is an operative field."[35] If we transpose Deleuze's reflections on figuration in visual art to what happens in *The Sportswriter*, we see a similar effect. There, the "person" Frank is "painted" against and onto a "place" that is as nondescript and floating as many of the "places" in Bacon's paintings are. In both cases, place is rendered diffuse and difficult to discern clearly, yet they isolate the figure and its explorations within the "circus ring," or onto itself. In the case of Ford's representation of Frank, this dynamic works in two ways: it not only brings about the figure orchestrated around Frank as hero but also serves to isolate isolation. In the awkward relationship between Frank's apathetic, dreamy, lost, and anesthetized response and the equally apathetic and lost suburban backdrop (the oval shape, the grids), the figure of solitude materializes in its "long empty moment."

Frank's fate is not quite that of Bartleby. Frank does, after all, surface out from under the film, and he does not choose *not* to participate. However, the immobility that both characters share turns them both into statue-like emblems of the stationary and indifferent. Bartleby drives his employer mad with what seems to the latter an utter lack of interest in and concern for his surroundings, and Frank's similar apathy gets on the reader's nerves. Herein also lies a stark critique of this particular manifestation of the imaginary's arrangement: staged as suburban ideal, one of the American imaginary's second-order institutions, organized into the homogenized and homogenizing suburban landscape. A most effective articulation of a response would be the figuration of the institution's, and on a different level, the whole imaginary's, cancellation, which is not so much open defiance and refusal as just immobility and resignation, the neglect of further aspiration. To return to Beuka's observation, noted at the beginning of this chapter, that suburban communities are "places that might be read, in geographer Yi-Fu Tuan's terminology, as 'landscapes of fear,'" we could perhaps modify this and suggest that it is not fear as much as resignation and immobility that are the characteristics. For it is important to note that resignation, not rebellion, poses as aspiration's opposite.

In light of the foregoing, if the sustenance of the imaginary relies on transference, or, in tropological terms, metaphoricity, the dynamics of crossing conceptually discreet spheres of meaning and reference, then a position such as that represented in *The Sportswriter* is anchored in metonymically circumscribed and unyielding pockets of meaning and reference. That constellation brings us into a slightly different area, the potential conflict between the drive of transference and forward orientation, and the static and retrospectively oriented. Herein lies the variance of transculturation and transvaluation that was discussed in chapter 1 and that I consider in two diametrically opposed contexts in the following chapter. For in order to gauge the sway of the imaginary, the places where it runs up against limitations must also be considered.

[5]

"RELATIONS STRETCHED OUT" IN THE AMERICAN IMAGINARY

DOREEN MASSEY'S observation that "The spatial is social relations stretched out" sounds simple, yet when we stop to think through what those words actually mean, the statement presents phenomenal complexities. In light of the remark, the truism that America is a nation of immigrants takes on a more convoluted and intricate significance, since its history is the history of the "simultaneity of stories-so-far,"[1] of the interrelations between spaces and trajectories that have been woven together across continents and centuries, yet have been sustained in actual space, within national borders. The discussion of Whitman and Gonzales from chapter 3 revealed that, on critical, epistemological, and culturological levels, these heterochronistic refractions bring out different and competing representations of the same space. They tie in with the full significance of Massey's simple phrasing. Consequently, within the American imaginary, there are a number of subimaginaries, feeding precisely on the dynamics of stretched-out relations. These are commonly and most obviously epitomized by second-order institutions such as immigrant and ethnic neighborhoods and organizations, which display varying degrees of customs, language, and practices from places of origin far away. They exist within, and in greater or lesser degrees of harmony with, the flexible and commanding founding ideas of transference and transformation. They are in themselves radical proofs of those very principles. In this chapter I consider the representation of such "relations stretched out" in two different contexts and two different manifestations. Distinct in form and culture as they are, they paradoxically mirror each other, and both speak powerfully to the transportation and persistence of imaginary institutions. They are Ana Menéndez's short story collection *In Cuba I Was a German Shepherd* and the cultural history of a small region in southern Norway.

Menéndez's stories are for the most part set in Miami, a city that "considers itself too American to be Cuban and too Cuban to be American."[2] At once on the inside and on the outside of the American imaginary, the characters in *In Cuba* are thus lodged in a symbolic sphere neither here nor there. The engagement with the American sphere is only nominal and seeps into the narratives mainly as an external gaze. The main catalyst for the institution of this liminal space within the American imaginary is Domino Park, which functions as a small piece of "living" Cuban history. This type of representation or mapping of cultural space operates according to principles of synecdoche and metonymy and is allowed to exist within the powerful metaphorical circumference of the master imaginary's call for progress and transformation. I suggest that the very fact of this metonymic phenomenon reaffirms the accommodating nature of the American imaginary, and that the example here allegorizes other subimaginaries existing on the fringes of the larger one. In the discussion of Menéndez's stories it is pertinent to revisit the "long empty moment" of Richard Ford's *The Sportswriter* in this connection, for not only is metonymy lonely, its mode's capacity for conservation and containment is also markedly potent in real life.

This is certainly the case in the other "case study" of this chapter, even if the history of the Lister region in southern Norway takes on a more synecdochic tinge and spatializing modality. Here we have an instance of a literal, not literary, institution of the American imaginary. The actual case shows the transposition of elements from the American imaginary in a reversed and selective process by which what pertains at the outset to the symbolic sphere is instituted elsewhere as, again, a piece of "living" history. In a faint echo of the triad of translation, transculturation, and transvaluation that we saw manifested in the Lithuanian's grasping of the extended promise in chapter 1, the Lister case divulges something about the capacity for transference that the American imaginary possesses, as well as about the acts of remembering and selecting in processes of cultural bridging and representation. While in the Lithuanian's case transvaluation takes place in an orientational mode that moves toward the culturological inside of the imaginary, the Lister case elucidates the reverse, the movement of the cultural inside toward spheres of reception and resonance elsewhere. Both Menéndez's short stories and the history of Lister can, ultimately, be read as commentaries on modalities of migration as these are mapped out in memory and in scripture, in fiction or in concrete sociocultural arrangements.

The Cultural Imaginary of "Greater Cuba": Suspended

The eleven short stories in Ana Menéndez's *In Cuba I Was a German Shepherd* (2001) are highly varied in theme and narrative voice: they relate communication breakdowns in relationships, the sudden overflow of bananas in a backyard, a homecoming party, a boyhood dream of grandeur, dark fears at night before the next surveillance flight, and growing old and lonely, to mention some of the topics. The book reads like a loosely assembled snapshot album, where some characters make appearances in several stories, and others only once. Some, such as Raúl and Máximo in the title story, reappear in two other stories within the same time frame, and so do Raúl's son Anselmo, his wife Meegan, the young girl Mirta, Felipe, and his wife Hortencia, who should have been an actress. Most of the stories are set in Miami, some with Máximo's restaurant as their main reference point. A few are set in Cuba. The details of locations, however, are of less importance, because all the stories are informed by and relate to an imaginary that transcends the actual border between the United States and Cuba. We recall here Castoriadis's definition of the imaginary as: "the unceasing and essentially *undetermined* (social-historical and psychical) creation of *figures/forms/images*, on the basis of which alone there can ever be a question of something. What we call 'reality' and 'rationality' are its works."[3] In a manner similar to Américo Paredes's coinage of "Greater Mexico," that is, the culturally shared space on both sides of the U.S.-Mexican border, the space that constitutes the background for Menéndez's narratives can be construed as that of

"Greater Cuba," a social imaginary transcending geopolitical boundaries. Regarding the concept of Greater Mexico, Norma Klahn observes that clear-cut demarcations between the spaces of the Mexicana and the Chicana cannot be made; they are too closely linked by and within an imaginary that crosses the border: "Re-adapted to specific circumstances and political realities, [symbols from the Mexican imaginary] acquire new meanings that symbolically destabilize the traditional perceptions of peoples in the new geo-symbolic/imagined space of Mexicanness and outside geographic boundaries."[4] This is not to say that there are not differences between the American and Mexican sides of the border (or the American and Cuban). The identification of how these are interlinked, accommodated, and sometimes misappropriated is indeed the focus of Klahn's essay, and similar caution must also be applied to the consideration of other, similarly shared spaces.

It may be useful here to recall Charles Taylor's general definition of the imaginary as "the ways in which people imagine their social existence, how they fit together with others, how things go on between them and their fellows, the expectations that are normally met, and the deeper normative notions and images that underlie these expectations."[5] If we read this alongside Cornelius Castoriadis's emphasis on the "(social-historical and psychical) creation of *figures/forms/images*," and with a view to shared spaces that cross borders, the question arises, how do such figures and images find expression? One could argue that such "greater" imaginaries are not essentially different from any other social imaginary. However, an extra dimension is added to the dissemination processes in cases of diasporas: cultural groups are separated by sometimes vast geographical and social differences, yet are bound in a temporal continuity of shared expectations and norms. In these circumstances it is not a given that the social imaginary coincides with the cultural one, and the saloonkeeper's daughter's conversion to the American imaginary is not always possible. Clearly, given political and social history, the imaginary of Greater Mexico displays a certain amount of convergence between the social and cultural constituents, as the discussion of Gonzales's "I am Joaquín" in chapter 3 showed. One might object that a distinction between the two categories, social and cultural, cannot be made, since any given culture creates its forms and images according to moral and ethical underpinnings specific to itself. However, the numerous cultural enclaves around the world that are loyal to and serve as extensions of "mother imaginaries" elsewhere clearly operate on a double level of imaginary relations. If the social imaginary is the manner in which participants in and of a given imaginary co-inhabit their shared space, then perhaps the cultural imaginary infuses this on the level of modality. If the American master imaginary aspires to unify manner and modality into one on the axis of metaphorical transference, then a number of subimaginaries can be localized as metonymically or synecdochically marked by their anchoring in "elsewhere." However, the divergence between social and cultural as a divergence between manner and modality need not be inherently unbridgeable; in most cases it is not.

In the following exploration of Menéndez's *In Cuba*, I examine how the creative and re-creative function of an imaginary "elsewhere" generates and upholds figures and forms in narratives outside the social and cultural imaginary in which they are in fact located. Moreover, I pursue this in relation to figurative modes and their prefigurative moments, and suggest that what surfaces in Menéndez's stories is a consistency of the metonymic mode, with the American imaginary's core of transference and transformation in the metaphorical as a barely noticeable presence. The persistence of such subimaginaries within the larger American one underscores a factor of cultural life that goes to the heart of debates over multiculturalism and integration and that, regardless of context, perhaps speaks to the particular version of the migratory that is driven by extreme inevitability.

To appreciate Menéndez's work, however, it is necessary briefly to look at certain aspects of the generic tradition that it can be read into. The interlocking of multiple characters and destinies that characterizes this collection is not uncommon, certainly not in Latino literature. For instance, we find it in Puerto Rican Nicolasa Mohr's *In Nueva York*, in Mexican-American Sandra Cisneros's *Woman Hollering Creek*, and in Tomás Rivera's . . . *And the Earth Did Not Devour Him*. These are all short story collections that, because of partially or completely recurrent characters or themes, can also be read as novels. Such snapshot works can furthermore be read as community novels that aspire to narrate and chronicle characters and episodes as they are connected communally. The strategy is to consolidate, socially and culturally, a place for the collective self within the larger society and its imaginary, rather than to focus on the individual subject per se. The thread of coherence that enables these sustained, novelistic readings is generated by a spatial and temporal consistency in terms of narrative space. Mohr's characters, for instance, all exist in the novel's spatially present moment, as do those of Cisneros and Rivera. Despite frequent moments of retrospection, which add narrative depth in all these texts, the reader never loses sight of the continuum that situates the characters within a shared spatial perspective.

The situation is rather different in *In Cuba*. Certainly, as I mentioned previously, there are connections between some characters and stories. And yet relationships that would generate a sense of communality and its assertion within the space of the larger context seem absent, or too weak to create coherence. What instead distinguishes this collection of stories is an orientational predisposition that unsettles spatial and temporal unity. On the one hand, this characteristic frustrates attempts at continuous relations between characters, between cultures and nations, and between what Bal calls the experience of heterochrony within individual characters, in that it "disrupts the traditional linear narratives onto which routine responses and images are grafted, it offers temporal shelter to memories."[6] In this sense, the short story collection should be read simply as a collection of independent stories, loosely held together by a certain number of reappearances. On the other hand, that very same fragmentation also provides an insistent thematic coherence and emerges as a powerful connecting figure in and of itself, by providing the shelter necessary for remembering "elsewhere," and other times. Since what Castoriadis refers to as "*figures/forms/images*" are created in and by the imaginary, in this case of what we may call Greater Cuba, they exist on both sides of the water, which in several of the stories sometimes makes it hard to say exactly where they are set. Most importantly, the figures and forms are fuelled by what is elsewhere, or better stated, the memory of that "elsewhere." This absent presence, or present absence, runs through the entire collection of stories and generates only a nominal engagement with actual surroundings, instead consolidating the parameters of its own inside. The function of memory is crucial in forging the aesthetics in both this text and the township in Norway we return to later.

In her analyses of *The Brothers Karamazov*, Dianne Thompson observes that "The continuity of memory makes us unite what dissimilarity (spatio-temporal) might otherwise separate; similarity makes us unite what discontinuity in the memory might hold apart."[7] This is particularly relevant to narratives of the migratory, for while they are not inherently different from other literatures, they uniquely intensify the sensitivity to the temporal and spatial complexities and contradictions embedded in all attempts at representation. The first story in Menéndez's collection is an excellent illustration of this. The story gives the book its title, and I concentrate on it here. It is set in a little park in Miami where older men come to play dominos, hence the name Domino Park. The main characters are Máximo and Raúl, both Cuban, and Carlos and Antonio, who are from the Dominican Republic. The park plays a pivotal role in their lives and is introduced in the first paragraph as follows:

> The park where the four men gathered was small. Before the city put it on its tourist maps, it was just a fenced rectangle of space that people missed on the way to their office jobs. The men came each morning to sit under the shifting shade of a banyan tree, and sometimes the way the wind moved through the leaves reminded them of home.[8]

The second sentence refers to the actual history of the park, which was closed down for a period because of drug trafficking. The passage thus hints at and problematizes the park's present status as a gentrified tourist attraction, which has made Máximo reluctant to visit it: "He had seen the rows of tourists pressed up against the fence, gawking at the colorful old guys playing dominos. 'I'm not going to be the sad spectacle in someone's vacation slide show,' he said."[9] When he becomes a widower with empty days to fill, however, he starts frequenting the park with his old friend from Havana, Raúl, and after a while they start playing against Antonio and Carlos:

> For many months they didn't know much about each other, these four men. Even the smallest boy knew not to talk when the pieces were in play. But soon came Máximo's jokes, during the shuffling. . . . And the four men learned to linger long enough between sets to color an old memory while the white pieces scraped along the table.[10]

Máximo gets into the habit of telling jokes during shuffling. They all refer to Cuba, to Fidel Castro; always lingering beneath the laughter is the sadness of no return. We shall look at the jokes more closely later on. On the surface, the plot centers on Máximo's interaction with the small community of domino players. This takes us to the day when his already ambivalent relationship to the park's touristy character becomes a crisis. The park itself is highly ambiguous in its instance as a culturological metaphor. In its previous form, the park existed as a cultural manifestation in its own right, as a synecdochic representation of Cuba. It was there as a part standing for the whole, alleviating its visitors' pain of dislocation and exile, a condition that in Spanish is significantly named *desterrado*, "unearthed." Domino Park thus forms an imaginary bridge back into the country that was lost, a figure created by and in the imaginary of Greater Cuba that in turn institutes itself into and as an actual place. This instance, albeit fictionally represented, is an illustration of how the human mind seeks understanding by relating the unknown to what is already known, or, as Michael Seidel puts it, "Imaginative powers begin at the boundaries of accumulated experience."[11] Tales from and of the migratory therefore always entail a certain amount of figuration, and the migrant who faces a new world must rely on an ability to map the world that lies in front of him or her so that it becomes inhabitable. These are basic mechanics of comprehension, and they involve a number of cognitive processes. Hayden White writes of:

> rendering the unfamiliar, or the "uncanny" in Freud's sense of that term, familiar; of removing it from the domain of things felt to be "exotic" and unclassified into one or another domain of experience encoded

> adequately enough to be felt to be humanly useful, non-threatening, or simply known by association. This process of understanding can only be tropological in nature, for what is involved in the rendering of the unfamiliar is a troping that is generally figurative.[12]

Healing the epistemological rifts created by dislocation and relocation, bridging the gaps opened up by spatiotemporal dissimilarities and ruptures, requires the activation and engagement of memory on a fundamental and practical level, in order to project one experiential domain onto another. Consequently, what cognitive linguists call metaphorical mapping and what White calls "troping" in the passage just cited are essentially the same thing: understanding through oscillation between conceptual meanings. From a cognitive point of view, metaphorical mapping is more specifically the mapping of a source domain that differs experientially from the target domain onto which it is mapped. The basic structure of the target domain remains intact.[13] In other words, the unfamiliar structure onto which a familiar domain is projected does not undergo fundamental change but becomes a coating of new codes and configurations—and hence more or less new meanings.

Cognitive linguistics and tropology enter into this discourse from very different places, but they share the conviction that the faculty of imagination or figuration is the modus operandi for orientation in the world. White puts it as follows: "Thought about the physical world remains essentially figurative . . . progressing by all sorts of 'irrational' leaps and bounds from one theory to another."[14] In a similar vein, Antonio Barcelona asserts that "one of the major general abilities is imagination, or in more technical terms, the ability to project concepts onto other concepts."[15] Both restate Castoriadis's conceptualization of radical imagination as "the ability to symbolize. . . . to see a thing in another thing."[16] Troping is essential to maneuvering in the world, and its practice manifests itself culturologically in one form or another, on all levels, wherever people from different cultures inhabit the same space. Language, custom, religion, and tradition all undergo a certain degree of figuration as they travel from one domain to another. The results (with exceptions that are many and tragic) are blends that tend to emerge as distinct domains with the potential to generate other blends. Sometimes cognition is trapped in a schema of figuration that the imagination cannot escape. Rather than translating and familiarizing the unknown and new, which would create new metaphors, the imagination remains within a tropological model and modality that do not allow such a transfusion.

In the case of Máximo and Domino Park as a culturological figuration, the processes of gentrification and touristification not only have changed the park's surface but have altered its very gestalt. American Miami, which in cognitive terms would correspond to the source domain, has "mapped" its experiential structure onto the park (corresponding to the target domain). What was once a part *for* the whole has been turned into a part *of* a whole, and now of a very different domain. Even if the basic structure of the part (as a place to go and play dominos) is retained, at least on the surface, its synecdochic significance to the Cuban community is profoundly destabilized. The domino players are now outsiders and visitors in a domain that has been appropriated by an outside perspective. Máximo cannot quite reconcile himself to this new gestalt and senses the whole situation as both humiliating and irritating:

> The tour groups arrived in later that afternoon. First the white buses with the happy blue letters WELCOME TO LITTLE HAVANA. Next, the fat women in white shorts, their knees lost in an abstraction of flesh. Máximo tried to concentrate on the game.
>
> "You see, Raúl," Máximo said. "You see how we're a spectacle?" He felt like an animal and wanted to growl and cast about behind the metal fence.[17]

The analogy to a zoo leaves no doubt that Máximo senses acutely that he is being robbed of both his own and the park's autonomy. Whether it is this emotion or the hot sun that makes him physically sick is uncertain, but, following the sensation of being an animal caught in a cage, he begins to feel strange. This is further exacerbated by the episode that immediately follows, an insertion into the narrative of the perspective of the surrounding American imaginary that is oblivious to nontransference:

> An open trolley pulled up and parked on the curb. A young man with blond hair, perhaps in his thirties, stood up in the front, holding a microphone. He wore a guayabera.[18] Máximo looked away.
>
> "This here is Domino Park," came the amplified voice in English, then Spanish. "No one under fifty-five allowed, folks. But we can sure watch them play."
>
> Máximo heard shutters click, then convinced himself he couldn't have heard, not from where he was.
>
> "Most of these men are Cuban and they're keeping alive the tradition of their homeland," the amplified voice continued, echoing against the back wall of the park. "You see, in Cuba, it was very common to retire to a game of dominos after a good meal. It was a way to bond and build community. Folks, what you are seeing here is a slice of the past. A simpler time of good friendships and unhurried days."[19]

Máximo's unease is palpable, and, thinking that "he could no longer sit where he was, accept things as they were," he has a fit of uncontrollable anger and tries to attack the guide.[20] The scene conjures up complex and painful cultural interactions, reactions, and finally actions. On the one hand, the domino players are enacting a ritual that at the outset seeks to ignore the framework of American Miami and retain the symbolic and instituted meanings of Cuba, of home. Upon hearing the guide talk, however, an absurdly similar point of perception sneaks in as a twisted echo of Máximo's own framework. The guide correctly presents the park—and Máximo—in terms of their roles within Greater Cuba, but does so from outside its imaginary and corresponding institutions, approaching them instead as dead objects, musealized parts of the whole.

As a reversed process of figuration, this takes its cue from an external point of view literally looking in, construing the scene as a "slice of the past," a synecdoche again, but in a different sense. This point of perception appropriates as its own the right (and rite) of troping. It may be that the guide's discourse reflects an aestheticization of the park and its ritual as emblematic of a specific culture's practices, but this is ultimately an act of objectification that robs the object of its own perception and its own seriousness. In other words, this mapping projects a perspective that retains its object of perception as fundamentally other and alien to its own culturological inside.

What is striking about the transformation of the park is that, even if the point of perception changes and the direction of troping is reversed, the untranslatability of the two referential domains remains constant. Neither points of perception nor their interactions with their objects are instances of metaphorical mappings in the sense of domain *crossings*. Synecdoches are not transgressional; they insist on keeping intact their miniature versions of the larger phenomenon they seek to represent. Instead, the park, in both its earlier and its present forms, is the manifestation of a different kind of border crossing that is more reminiscent of, for instance, Chinatowns. These phenomena do not illustrate troping as a process that produces new metaphors and icons such as La Virgen de Guadalupe or ethnically blended neighborhoods. Chinatowns (and Domino Park) exist in an imagined, one-to-one correspondence between old and new, between past and present, even if they become ossified, archaic versions that, paradoxically, are exotic to their mother imaginaries. The main characteristic of such demonstrations of figuration remains that they do not *significantly* traverse their own domain boundaries conceptually. What Thompson calls "spatio-temporal dissimilarities" are here cancelled out.

In his discussion of exilic writing and the *Odyssey*, Michael Seidel describes this dynamic as one whereby "the expression of the desire for home becomes a substitute for home." Odysseus's exilic adventures, he continues, "[are attempts] to dim the hero's homeward compulsion by making exilic space a substitute for the home island." By replacing home with its replica, Odysseus "displays not only the full range of exilic course, extension and return, but the full power of exilic imagining, *extension as return.*"[21] Troping, as we see it played out in the relationship between Domino Park and its surroundings, is an expression of precisely such a desire for replication and extension, not for transformation. It therefore bears the mark of metonymy rather than metaphor.

Metonymy has been granted less attention than metaphor by cognitive linguistics. This may be because metonymy quickly runs up against its own borders; unlike metaphor, metonymy carries a certain finality. In Barcelona's definition, metonymy is "[a] conceptual projection whereby one experiential domain (the target) is partially understood in terms of another experiential domain (the source) included in the same common experiential domain. Metonymy is . . . activation."[22] This description bears on Domino Park and its role, from the perspectives of both the tourists and the Cubans. Metonymic figuration rejects significant experiential domain crossing and retains a preference for the contiguity of parts closely relating to wholes. Metonymic memory in turn selects what it remembers along a continuous line on which one can imagine one item or function standing very close to another.[23]

This is a relation, a mode of ordering, whose structure is located in a prior discursive operation, in processes of prefiguration that come before mental activities of troping. We can suggest that exile's orientation is not to make the new and unfamiliar home and familiar; home is forever lost somewhere else—a frozen image that obsesses memory. As a circumstance that prefigures and orders discourse, exile therefore falls into a specific tropological structure whose main component cannot be metaphor: domain crossing is not an adequate mode for constituting its object of discourse. The orientation remains toward the past, and the obsession is not only with remembering but also with oblivion—or rather, the fear of oblivion.[24] The park and the scene that unfolds are refracted in Máximo's discourse as the mirroring of a certain kind of prefiguration along the general lines just described. This is circumscribed metonymically, and it constitutes and is constituted by the mode of exile: "The here of one in exile persistently recalls the space of a there, and vice versa. . . . Nothing in the land of exile seems to have its own self-contained unity. . . . the exile is by definition incomplete without the memory of a former existence, the necessary yet deceptive proof of his or her being."[25] It is therefore essential that memory stay with the same figure, a figure that describes and secures home, so as not to be lost altogether. Exile's obsession with the frozen image of somewhere else thus engages in a process of metonymically reproducing, or as Seidel puts it, extending, the figure (the memory) of home in an endless line of extensions.

As discussed in chapter 1, the social imaginary needs a multiplicity of encounters to stay vital, lest it become, as Bakhtin observes in relation to cultural domains in general, "vacuous, arrogant, degenerat[e] and d[ying]." We saw that the main forces driving the American imaginary are, roughly speaking, transference and transformation, the future orientation of a new cultural and social space that is created in and creates its own image, so to speak. This is, I have suggested, nowhere more evident than in the ideological currents that carry Walt Whitman's "Song of Myself," which institutes the imaginary's promise safely within the myth of progress. In the very few encounters that appear in Menéndez's stories, there is a marked distance and even impossibility of interaction between the two domains. The meeting between the guide, with his tourists, and the players in the park, serves as an example: by identifying the gestalt of the park as quaint and musealized, the guide's words locate the park firmly on the outside of the American imaginary from which he speaks. This is an encounter between metaphorical transference and metonymic detachment, between future orientation and the backward gaze.

Similar meetings between cultural, if not social, imaginaries also take place in Menéndez's "Hurricane Stories," which stages a conversation between two unnamed protagonists, a man and a woman, one late afternoon on a beach. As the woman speaks from inside the imaginary of Greater Cuba, her discourse is fraught with a poetics of memory that structures her part of the conversation, the story she is telling, and the associations that well up as she is remembering. By narrating stories, the young woman tries to hold on to her place in the man's life and mind: "I'm afraid if I stop talking, if I say something that makes his eyes narrow, that his love will disappear back into the folds of all those stories he hasn't told me." The two may be sitting next to each other; they may be in a relationship, but the woman's efforts seem futile: "He says he understands. But he grew up with snow in the winter and fir trees against gray skies. I had Florida."[26] Florida and Havana are blurred, however, and hence in reality the unnamed woman refers to the present absence so tangible in all of the stories, and to which there is little access from the outside.

That "to be displaced is to be obsessed with memory" is also made amply clear in other parts of Máximo's story.[27] Consider for instance the following passage:

> After several glasses of wine, someone would start the stories that began with "In Cuba I remember." They were stories of old lovers, beautiful and round-hipped. Of skies that stretched on clear and blue to the Cuban hills. Of green landscapes that clung to the red clay of Guines, roots dug in like fingernails in a good-bye. In Cuba, the stories always began, life was good and pure. But something always happened to them in the end, something withering, malignant. Máximo never understood it. The stories that opened in the sun, always narrowed in a dark place.[28]

There are two principal figurations here. The first is the simile "roots dug in like fingernails in a good-bye," wherein the latter part is itself a metaphor that conjures up the despair of departure. The second is a figuration of story as movement, likening the narrativization of memory to a journey and spatializing and localizing its beginning and end. Figuration is, however, inherently unstable and inaccurate, if for no other reason than that absence of figure does not exist. No language is neutral, and even what is referred to as the zero-degree style is, as Genette puts it, merely "a sign defined by the absence of sign, the value of which is perfectly recognized."[29] In a wider sense, all figuration is "both a deviation from one possible, proper meaning, but also a deviation towards another meaning, conception, or ideal of what is right and proper and true 'in reality.'"[30] Its more specific operation, writes Genette, means that:

> Between the letter and the meaning, between what the poet has written and what he thought, there is a gap, a space, and like all space it possesses a form. This form is called figure, and there will be as many figures as one can find forms in the space that is created on each occasion between the line of the signifier . . . and that of the signified.[31]

The figure that surfaces in Máximo's description of storytelling after closing time can be named suspension, capturing a Janus-like obsession with memory and oblivion: it both connects Máximo with and separates him from his old home, and its figural presence is what Roland Barthes compares to "the motif of a hovering music."[32] Furthermore, suspension, prefigured by the exilic mode, finds its place in a metonymic architectonics of memory. By naming exile's desire and its opposite, loss, the figure of suspension also spatializes the tension between the increasingly frequent dreams and daydreams Máximo has and his actual, everyday life. These (day)dreams all center on his dead wife Rosa, and his recollections of when they were young. Sitting alone at the pine table in his small apartment, Máximo finds his mind increasingly drifting back to when they met, when their children were little, their years in Havana, when they were first living and working together in Miami. The intensity of these dreams is such that "he'd begun to see her at the kitchen table as she'd been at twenty-five."[33] Máximo spends more and more of his time living in a recuperated absence, thus creating for himself an existence that analogizes the inherent fictitiousness of exile itself:

> He saw her at thirty, bending down to wipe the chocolate off the cheeks of their two small daughters. And his eyes moved from Rosa to his small daughters. He has something he needed to tell them. He saw them grown up, at the funeral, crying together. He watched Rosa rise and do the sign of the cross. He knew he was caught in a nightmare, but he couldn't stop. He would emerge slowly, creaking out of the shower and there she'd be, Rosa, like before, her breasts round and pink from the hot water, calling back through the years. Some mornings he would awake and smell peanuts roasting and hear the faint call of the manicero pleading for someone to relieve his burden of white paper cones.[34] Or it would be thundering, the long hard thunder of Miami that was so much like the thunder of home that each rumble shattered the morning of his other life. He would awake, caught fast in the damp sheets, and feel himself falling backwards.[35]

The dream images are evocations of "somewhere else" and can be read as a series of synecdochic representations of that. In this sense they illustrate Jacobson's assertion that "the development of a discourse may take place along two different semantic lines: one topic may lead to another through their similarity or through their contiguity."[36] The images in the last part of the passage are particularly conspicuous in this respect. Rosa "calling back through the years," the "smell [of] peanuts roasting," the "call of the manicero," and "the thunder of home" are all parts of a whole, projections evoking pieces of Havana in the present spatiotemporality of a present absence, or an absent presence. This accumulation of synecdoches furthermore illustrates how "an exile is someone who inhabits one place and remembers or projects the reality of another."[37] The double orientation in Máximo's discourse generates a discursive tension that ultimately results in a conflation of the distinctions between Havana and Miami—then and now. For instance, in the phrase "each rumble shattered the morning of his other life," it is unclear what, precisely, "other" refers to. Máximo's "other life" is, consequently, his present life, but one constituted by suspension between places and between times, never quite coinciding with itself—and therefore never quite real.

This dissonance can also be heard in the story "The Perfect Fruit." The two protagonists here are Raúl, whom we recognize from Domino Park, and his wife Matilde. The story takes place in their house, interrupted by numerous regressions into a past that, we understand, haunts Matilde. It begins as she is trying to digest the probability that her son is going to marry a woman Matilde does not care for. She is standing in the kitchen, contemplating the banana trees in the backyard that Raúl planted eight years ago, foolishly, in her opinion. She had been angry with him at first, since the trees ruined the green of her nice even lawn, but "each day after that she thought less and less about the trees until they passed into a deep part of memory that was almost like forgetting."[38] The image of the trees receding into the dark shades of oblivion will become central, and, in fact, a prefiguration of a moment of collapse not entirely unlike Máximo's in "In Cuba I Was a German Shepherd." Just as the trees after all this time suddenly begin bearing fruit, Matilde's own past rushes in to haunt her in a different kind of offering.

We follow her over a few days, as she frantically makes all kinds of dishes from the bananas that overflow in the backyard. All of this is in preparation for the dinner where her son and his future wife will make the announcement of their engagement, which Matilde dreads. While she cooks she is also drawn back through the years to a past that she may have suppressed but that now returns relentlessly. The catalyst for this process is an old photograph of her and Raúl on their own wedding day. In it, there is also another woman. Minutes before their son and his future wife arrive for dinner, Matilde confronts Raúl with the long-forgotten picture:

> "This is my favorite photograph," Matilde continued, "because in it, for all time, is Adriana Monterrey leaning over you, her black hair spilling across your shoulder like a Spanish shawl."
>
> Raúl frowned and wrapped his arms about his stomach.
>
> "Do you remember Adriana, Raúl? Oh, she was beautiful. You must remember her. In this photograph, she was kissing you on the cheek. Of course, in friendship. But the camera caught the stars in your eyes. I've never seen you as happy since. That smile!"[39]

The image is frozen in Matilde's mind in two different ways. The moment that the picture refers to carries a crisis, and at the same time this crisis is eternalized by having been photographed. This reflects Roland Barthes's observation on photography that "it is the absolute Particular, the sovereign Contingency, matte and somehow stupid, the This (this photograph, and not Photography), in short, what Lacan calls the *Túche*, the Occasion, the Encounter, the Real, in its indefatigable expression."[40] The absolute Particular in its never-changing form, moreover, embodies what Lacan elsewhere refers to as "the rails of metonymy," a perpetuation of a moment of encounter when Matilde sees frozen in time and in the mind the interception of her marriage. However, this event is a metonymy of another, more radical rupture that doubles the experience of dislocation. For the real breach comes later, when Matilde arrives in Miami with their infant son to join Raúl, only to discover the distance that has been created between them: "Raúl was in the back, next to the doors. But Matilde didn't shout out. When he turned, he looked first to Anselmo. They walked toward one another and finally Raúl hugged her, patting her back as someone comforting the sick. Anselmo began to cry." The gap is not bridged, and the photograph becomes its emblem: "We live alone in our own core, flitting over the surface now and then, pretending."[41]

Tropes of the Imaginary: "Little America" on the Outside

Rendering the unfamiliar familiar through tropological mapping of the kind I have described so far also occurs in more concrete culturological and cultural contexts. One may take as an example the turn Catholicism took in northern New Spain in 1531. The story is that the Virgin Mary appeared to Juan Diego in the shape of a brown Indian woman on the former site of an Aztec temple. The Roman Catholic Church eventually granted the appearance the status of a miracle, and from then on La Virgen de Guadalupe has been Mexico's and Mexicans' patron saint. To the indigenous people, however, the Virgin carried the elements of the ancient Aztec belief system that were necessary for a religious icon. The basic structure of the target domain (Roman Catholicism) was not fundamentally altered, but rather imposed upon and recoded by the source domain (Aztec religion). A similar metaphorization occurred in the transition to Christianity in Norway in the eleventh century, where some of the symbols on early church edifices display an unmistakably pagan character reminiscent of the decorations used on Viking ships. These architectural structures are, literally speaking, unchanged in their basic principles but adorned. Moreover, as hybrids, these new culturological metaphors are logical and successful outcomes of a process of figuration (or troping, or mapping) whereby understanding and acceptance occurs. Indeed, they are quite literal illustrations of transculturation. Domino Park in Menéndez's representation is not among these figurations; that is not its function. It is there to evoke and spatialize an "elsewhere."[42]

I turn now to the variations of such figuration in a concrete, nonliterary place. Lister is the name of a region in southern Norway, and, as is the case with so many other places around the world where cultures touch, traditions meet, and people live the realities of encounter, the locale illustrates a tropological orchestration influenced by "relations stretched out," strangely echoing the aforementioned choreography of "Greater Cuba" in Menéndez's fictional stories. I return to this peculiar dialectics and its meaning in relation to the American imaginary toward the end of this chapter. What follows now is the story of a "Little America."

When the shipping and fishing industries in southern Norway collapsed in the 1870s, whole villages left for the New World, as happened in so many other places in Europe around the same time. As a recent memorial in one of the villages in the Lister region reflects, the moment of saying farewell was marked by painful realizations that there might be no returning home. Depending on the weather and the ship, the southern Norwegians had between five and eight weeks to experience the Atlantic crossing as a physical transference in which daily sunsets and sunrises marked the passage of real time. Thus embodied, gazing up from the ship's deck at the slowly rotating skies, they were slowly distanced from their point of origin. Looking in from the outside gradually became a looking back, until the emigrant had become the immigrant, the change in status reflecting the transition from departure to arrival.

To the migrants from Lister, however, this modality was different, and notions of "home" and "not home" were kept spatially discreet yet temporally unified. These migrants never really left: their gaze was always turned back toward their home on the other side of the ocean, in a now-familiar pattern of work migration. In effect, they avoided having to choose between looking in and looking out, between departure and arrival. Instead, they created a middle space where their position in relation to the boundary between "home" and "away" was inherently temporary. Also, their engagement with and negotiation of the American imaginary as enabling filter were different; they were not aspiring to become full participants in it. In Europe, only Ireland saw more of its people leave for the United States than did Norway, and in this already extreme situation the Lister region, in the Vest Agder province in the south of the country, was among the areas that sent the most. Specifically, the transition from sailing ships to steamships in the 1880s and the ensuing recession in the coastal areas, which aggravated the preexisting impoverishment caused by population increase and exhausted farmland, finally forced people to leave. Emigration from

Lister started relatively late in the Norwegian context, but when it really got going, the population in local townships quickly decreased. In the 1920s, 34 percent of people born in Lister were in the United States; in some villages, more than half of the population had at one point or another made the crossing. Even to people who stayed behind and never made the passage themselves, names like Brooklyn, Chicago, New York, and New Jersey were often far more relevant and meaningful reference points in their everyday lives than were Olso, Bergen, and Trondheim, the largest Norwegian cities. Even if most of the sojourners stayed in the United States, many more returned than anywhere else in the country, and work migration continued longer in Lister than in most other places. In 1920, a full 26 percent of the "out-wandered" had returned for good, whereas in other provinces the percentage of remigration was as low as 3 percent. A local historian explains that:

> Already at the end of the 1880s it was apparent that the emigration from Agder to America had a different character than the emigration from the inland. The southerners participated in creating a new emigrant tradition that considered the States as a temporary work market, where one could save up money. . . . If it was necessary, the father in the house went over to the U.S. for a period of 2–3 years, while the wife and the kids ran the small farm at home.[43]

This pattern can to a significant extent be ascribed to a preexisting tradition in these southern areas of sailing and taking temporary work abroad. As early as the seventeenth century, people from the coastal parts of the region had gone to Holland in order to earn better livings as sailors and housemaids, and a tradition and culture of going abroad to work had been established at an early time. Consequently, these seafaring communities could draw on an old and familiar habit and tradition in their journeys to the United States. Already, after the peak in the 1920s, the pattern of work migration had become notorious: men left their homes, determined to come back after a few years, often taking the oldest son with them on their last trip, to set him up before they themselves retired. From that point onward, we can speak of commuter traffic between Lister and, for the most part, Brooklyn and Chicago, even if the migrants also went to Duluth to work in the forests, to Alaska to work in the gold mines, and to Tacoma and Seattle. Wherever they went, however, few settled on the land, and the following recollection from an elderly remigrant to Kvinesdal suggests that a great many of the emigrants from the Lister region left with a distinct objective of returning:

> When I 40 years ago traveled through the large Norwegian settlements in Wisconsin, Iowa, Minnesota, and Dakota, I could find reasonably pure Vossebygder, Sognebygder, Hallingsbygder and Valdresbygder,[44] but never did I find entire townships or communities of people from Agder [the province that Lister and Kvinesdal are located in]. They did not put their mark on the village. People from Vest Agder love their homes more than most.[45]

Young men left in the spring and returned around Christmas with a year's salary to show for themselves, much as seasonal workers do everywhere. The former Norwegian consul general in San Diego Oswald Gilbertson was part of this commuter traffic. He recalls in his memoirs that:

> Many of the emigrants in the 1960s became commuters. They worked hard for two to three years and saved their money. They returned to Kvinesdal, built a house, a barn, bought farms and land. When the money ran out they took another trip. These commuters had an enormous influence on the community economy.[46]

The traffic between the United States and Kvinesdal continued into the 1960s and 1970s but has since subsided. An economic upswing in the home country and thus in Lister made it unnecessary to leave. Indeed, many who at this point lived in the United States returned to find good jobs at home, especially in the offshore oil industry. However, the legacies of the intimate relationship that once existed between the two worlds remain very much alive. Most families still have close relatives in the United States, and many young men still go over to work with uncles and cousins or more distant relatives for shorter periods of time, especially in the construction business, even now. The local travel agency in Kvinesdal is called, not surprisingly, "The USA-Expert," and the manager explains that "It was established in 1969 precisely because of the traffic between America and Kvinesdal. Many of those who had emigrated now returned to the old country. The father in the house, however, would often commute between the U.S. and Norway, since the wages were still higher there and jobs were easier to find."[47] The persistent contact between old and new produced a curious and culturally idiosyncratic locale, where architecture, language, habits, and traditions from both places blended into each other over time, as a literal exemplification of "relations stretched out" into a classic example of a contact zone. Because these legacies have continued to exist on intimately personal and individual levels, they have proven strong and enduring, and the past thrives in the present in a variety of concrete, tangible, and, most importantly, dynamic ways. The physical downtown in Kvinesdal may be among the most striking illustrations of the actual institutionalization of symbolic carryover from the history of American sojourns. The typical southern Norwegian town is, by steadfast regional tradition, characterized by small, white-painted, wooden houses lining narrow streets and alleys. This architectural aesthetic is a source of pride and, of course, a tourist attraction, to the occasional despair of innovative people who do not have a cultural or personal connection and commitment to that same tradition. In the township of Kvinesdal, however, what resembles a wide main street runs between two rows of stores and houses, with each side having what seems to have been intended as parking space. This accommodation of vehicles gives away the off-beat identity of this small town, and, whether or not the layout can be traced to a culture of cars, the work migrants did bring all kinds of things American back with them, among them vehicles. As the community thrived on the money brought back from the United States, the development of the downtown presumably adapted to habits related to driving, which the infrastructure of the white-painted classic town could not handle.

Another somewhat related landmark also reveals this influence: overlooking the downtown, from one of the hillsides surrounding the valley, there used to be a medium-sized hotel, which I always suspected was the only real motel in Norway. It was torn down in

2009, but when I began working on this book it was still there. I decided to ask a local historian about its genesis. He turned out to be the original owner's nephew and brought out a little pamphlet in which his uncle had written the story of the hotel. "In February/March of 1961," the uncle writes, "I undertook a journey to the U.S. to visit four siblings and other relatives who lived there. I also wanted to spend as much time as possible traveling around the country to take a closer look at and study something I had only read about, namely the building and running of motels."[48]

These are among the more obvious testimonies to the concrete cultural influences that America has exerted on this small southern Norwegian community. It may be, however, that the less conspicuous ones, the bizarre details, tell us more profoundly how the imaginary travels. I used to live in one of these villages as a kid, and while I did not think much about it then, I remember well the kids who started school each fall. They had names like Mary Ann and Stanley, Samuel and Steven and Arleen, and they sometimes spoke a funny kind of Norwegian. Some only spoke English. But there was nothing unusual about this, about friends who spoke English at home, about their cars with wooden doors, the coming from and going to America of older siblings. More memorable and spectacular, at least to a child, were the amazing Christmas decorations. In the 1970s Norwegian Christmas traditions tended to be modest and simple, but not in Lister. There were reindeer with blinking eyes and noses on the roofs, big fluorescent Santas in the gardens, strings of lights on the trees. I was transfixed, and I never saw anything like that until twenty years later, when I spent my first Christmas in the United States. It was only when I moved away that I realized I was using words that no one outside of my village understood: they were English words phonetically pronounced in Norwegian, "trunk," "sink," "strit" (street), and Norwegian words weirdly diphthongized. Gilbertson calls this mix "Brooklynesian," describing it as the Norwegian language complemented by English words that received idiosyncratic pronunciation.[49] He too notes that for years he thought they were normal Norwegian words.

In 2010 the township of Kvinesdal built a bridge across the river, and to celebrate its opening, middle school students and their teachers performed a line dance to Alan Jackson's "Good Time." A fair number wore cowboy hats. As a spectator who is familiar with the feelings and practices that define this community, I was not really surprised, and I rather enjoyed the festivities—hats, music, and all. At the same time the ease and naturalness of the performance itself were quite striking; it did not seem like an artificial staging in any way, or like a performance of forgotten traditions evoked on special occasions, a slice of a musealized past. No, this very much seemed like an integrated production, matter-of-factly looked upon as a suitable way of honoring the opening of a bridge. The event makes a remarkable contrast with similar but reversed commemorations in, for instance, Norwegian communities in Minnesota and Wisconsin, where retrievals of the signatures of the Norwegian imaginary are performed as precisely musealized pieces of symbolism, unhinged from the flow of lived time and often exaggerated beyond recognition.

However, watching the line dance was also a partly unsettling reminder of other, less charming elements of cultural identifications that arise from "relations stretched out" in the township. Among the young dancers, a boy was wearing a t-shirt with the notorious Confederate flag splayed all over the chest, not knowing, one presumes, the associations the image continues to evoke in those who know its history. Or perhaps it was deliberate, for the flag vividly brings to mind instances of local vigilante justice when the police have been run out of town, the episodes of gun violence, the not entirely rare moments when the same Confederate flag has flown on the back of a pick-up truck, the unflinching love of a certain strand of country-and-western music, and a "Texan" self-reliance. Indeed, the master of ceremonies did jokingly refer to the township as "Little Texas," a further specification of this Little America that I shall return to.

All of these examples present different and varied aspects whose full culturological significance is noticeable only when you have a certain inside knowledge. While all small places everywhere trail shadows of local traditions and practices peculiar to their own genealogies, it is hard in this case to overlook the pressures from such genealogies elsewhere. The tropological orchestration of Domino

Park in Menéndez's story, set against the backdrop of Greater Cuba, is not essentially different from the example of Little America (or Little Texas) in southern Norway. The motel on the hillside that until recently overlooked the main street spatializes into existence the idea or the image of something far away, in the same way that the park performs its role of enacting an imaginary elsewhere. However, in the case of this Little America, the question is, what is being (tropologically) enacted?

Although the majority of the work migrants commuted between southern Norwegian villages and metropolitan centers such as Chicago and New York, what transpires in actual translation is generally an all-American small town, and more specifically one filtered through an interpretation of the Southwest. It is worth repeating Castoriadis's previously quoted observation that "The imaginary has to use the symbolic not only to 'express' itself (this is self-evident), but to 'exist', to pass from the virtual to anything more than this."[50] In a rather intricate turn of events, the passage between the American imaginary and the Kvinesdal township has followed a pattern of translation, transculturation, and transvaluation that has stayed notably faithful to that imaginary elsewhere. The problem, if we can call it that, is that the passing from virtual to "anything more than this" is the transiting of a particular kind of *interpretation*. This is not as much a mistranslation as a distillation, but, quite unlike the reverse order in the Minnesota example, in which Norwegian customs and traditions are sometimes reenacted almost *ad absurdum*, it corresponds to compatible and lived interpretations on the inside of the imaginary elsewhere. If the concept of the social imaginary enables the oscillation between the idea or ideal as an image of something and the real as it materializes in practices and understandings, then the concrete example of Lister brings that alternation into relief, and it does not matter if the elements do not match actual experience, if the local history is not grounded in Texan specificities.

The idea and ideal of the imaginary are what matters, and as the two travel across the Atlantic they are given a certain shape. If we now add that, as Terence Turner says, "'Synecdoche' may be defined, in general terms, as a specific relationship between metaphor and metonymy, as when a part of a whole (a metonymic relation) also replicates the form of the whole (a metaphoric relation)," the variance between the example of Little America or Little Texas in southern Norway and that of Greater Cuba in Menéndez's fictional setting is further clarified. It is a transculturated "form" of the American imaginary that passes from virtual (the idea of the small town) into "more than this," but it is the replication on a contiguous line of the Cuban imaginary that occurs in Domino Park. In both cases, the dynamic in the encounter with the American imaginary of transference takes us squarely back to Sacvan Bercovitch's analogy to chess and variations: if "America" is a middle game, and the old world (what is left behind) is an endgame, then the master trope of synecdoche is at once flexible and conceptually resistant enough to enable the kind of translations each example stands for.[51] However, the endgame variation could in this context be said to be carried out contiguously and retrospectively, a modality to which the backward-looking gaze of forced migration more easily conforms and that also shuts off the inherent metaphoricity of what Bercovitch describes as "continual movement toward endings that issues in an endless affirmation of beginnings."[52] "Beginnings" are not the point. As we saw, it is the return that matters.

The juxtaposition of these two very differently originated and constituted participations in the American imaginary underscores the figure of suspension that dominates the choreography of both as they carve into existence their respective versions of a living past. One is generated from the peculiarity of exile, the other from the increasingly common and global pattern of work migration. Suspension, however, not only shapes the actual institution of the subimaginary (the Cuban and the American out of place) but also determines the (minor) degree to which negotiation with the American imaginary is carried out. In each of these two cases, this occurs for wildly different reasons, but with curiously similar outcomes. In the case of Little America, I suggest that it is the cultural imaginary, not the social imaginary, that has been transposed and its idea and ideal instituted as the small town. In the case of Greater Cuba, it is the other way around: Menéndez's characters exist in the American social imaginary, but not in the cultural one. There is a definite split between the two, and these representations thus address the routes of other similar participants in the American imaginary (or any other "host" imaginary), who, by choice or by force, are excluded from transitioning into the schema of transference and mobility. This is also a part of the focus of the next and final chapter, which returns to the movie *Sugar* and the larger, more complex issues that center precisely on interpretations of the institution of the imaginary: whose imaginary is it?

[6]

RECALLING AMERICA: HUNTINGTON AND RODRIGUEZ

WE HAVE SEEN that the concept of the imaginary is a tool for gauging how various participants relate to, contest, and always, in some form or another, disseminate the tenets and currents that sustain the imaginary's flexible function as enabling filter. This is nowhere more evident than in the oscillation between what, from both the outside and the inside of this filter, is conceived of as the idea or ideal, Castoriadis's image *of* something, and the way this image materializes in actual understandings and practices, its institution. However, one also has to ask whether the numerous challenges to, responses to, and contestations of the master imaginary, in tandem with significant changes in the ethnic and cultural fabric, will in the end alter the filter. We therefore come to a slightly different and more general question concerning the nature of institution itself. How will the American social imaginary continue to uphold and be upheld by its constituent parts? Two works of nonfiction speak unexpectedly and poignantly to this question: Samuel Huntington's *Who Are We? The Challenges to America's National Identity* (2004) and Richard Rodriguez's *Brown: The Last Discovery of America* (2002). Even if neither author refers to the concept of the imaginary explicitly, they can be read as participants in a dialogue regarding its future. More particularly, their somewhat unlikely dialogue also reflects opposing perspectives on impulses of culturological conservation and essentialism that in the end move beyond the space of America.

In *Who Are We?* (the last book he wrote before he died in 2008), Huntington begins by posing a number of salient questions, essentially regarding the future of the American imaginary as I have explored that concept. In the following introductory passage he states:

> "We Americans" face a substantive problem of national identity epitomized by the subject of this sentence. Are we a "we," one people or several? If we are a "we," what distinguishes us from the "thems" who are not us? Race, religion, ethnicity, values, culture, wealth, politics, or what? Is the United States, as some have argued, a "universal nation," based on values common to all humanity and in principle embracing all peoples? Or are we a Western nation with our identity defined by our European heritage and institutions? Or are we unique with a distinctive civilization of our own, as the proponents of "American exceptionalism" have argued throughout our history? Are we basically a political community whose identity exists only in a social contract embodied in the Declaration of Independence and other founding documents? Are we multicultural, bicultural, or unicultural, a mosaic or a melting pot? Do we have any meaningful identity as a nation that transcends our subnational ethnic, religious, racial identities?[1]

Throughout *Who Are We?* Huntington, a social scientist perhaps best known for his influential and controversial *The Clash of Civilizations* from 1996, goes through a number of ways in which these questions can be probed, gauged, and responded to. He argues that the significance of the foundation of the United States in and as an English, dissenting, Protestant settler community cannot be ignored (he moves through a range of periods, events, trends, and societal categories, but space does not allow for a consideration here of any but his most central arguments). From that origin, Huntington argues, derive specific, salient traditions and cultural cores that to this day remain the underpinnings of the defining characteristics of the nation. The "American Creed," as Huntington's preferred term goes, is the product of the following elements:

> the English language; Christianity; religious commitment; English concepts of the rule of law, the responsibility of rulers, and the rights of individuals; and dissenting Protestant values of individualism, the work ethic, and the belief that humans have the ability and the duty to try to create a heaven on earth, a "city on a hill."[2]

These are values that originate in the settler colony, laying the foundations for later American, independent, national culture and identity, and, in various constellations and manifestations around the world, for a foreign political and at times imperialist agenda. Against the set of beliefs that secured national coherence for most of the nation's history, Huntington identifies a number of challenges and threats. As he says early on, the principal theme in *Who Are We?* is the "challenge to the continuing centrality of Anglo-Protestant culture to American national identity."[3] However, in most of the chapters it is the potential undermining of American cultural and societal integrity by Hispanic immigration in general and by Mexican immigration in particular that is repeated.

Four years before his book came out, Huntington published a short piece titled "The Special Case of Mexican Immigration," where he formulated the essence of the argument he would elaborate in the book. He concluded the article on the following note: "Mexican immigration looms as a unique and disturbing challenge to our cultural integrity, our national identity, and potentially to our future as a country."[4] While this piece went largely unnoticed, a longer article published in *Foreign Policy* in the spring of 2004 did not. Titled "The Hispanic Challenge," it argued that immigration from the south endangers American cultural unity and that, as the article begins, "The United States ignores this challenge at its peril."[5] Mexicans in particular are described as a menace to American national stability, to cultural coherence, and to the legacy of Anglo-Protestant founding beliefs, mostly because, Huntington argues, they differ from other immigrant groups throughout American history in certain basic ways. He categorizes these as contiguity, scale, illegality, regional concentration, persistence, historical presence, and language, to mention some of the most important headings:[6] "Unlike past immigrant groups, Mexicans and other Latinos have not assimilated into mainstream U.S. culture, forming instead their own political and linguistic enclaves—from Los Angeles to Miami—and rejecting the Anglo Protestant values that built the American dream."[7]

This argument, along with the publication shortly afterward of *Who Are We?* itself, attracted immediate attention. Many condemned both as conservative rants. For instance, in his article "Patriot Games," Louis Menand concluded that "either [Huntington's] book is a prescient analysis of trends obscure to the rest of us, or he has missed the point."[8] Even Alan Wolfe objected to what he called Huntington's "moralistic passion" and "hysteria," charges he later reiterated after a counterattack from Huntington that also appeared in *Foreign Policy*.[9] I will not go through all the criticisms and reviews that followed, but the *Nation* columnist Daniel Lazare concluded his review of the book on a note that is relevant to what I am pursuing here. Lazare observed that *Who Are We?*

> represents a return to the ideas of Edmund Burke, a longstanding hero of Huntington's, who argued that "a perfect democracy is . . . the most shameless thing in the world" and that a nation must be seen as a mystical union "between those who are living, those who are dead, and those who are to be born." The effect of such thinking is to reduce "we the living" to little more than "temporary possessors and life-renters," as Burke put it, and to substitute tradition for popular sovereignty. Instead of the present triumphing over the past, it means the past triumphing over the present.[10]

Lazare's critique gets at a problem that extends beyond Huntington's analysis of the future of his America, a question of whose culturological memory, whose route, and, finally, whose imaginary shall prevail. For Huntington's statement is really a call for a renewed commitment and pledge to the American Creed as he defines it, and while this is a perfectly legitimate position, it also dangerously evokes the ghosts of nativism and essentialism. Finally, of greatest relevance to the present discussion of the American imaginary, it seeks to stabilize, frame, and fix its enchantment of transference and to reroute its sway so that it carries specific, hardened elements. Paradoxically, the consequences of this maneuver are potentially antithetical to the America that Huntington sets out to recover and conserve.

The reflections and arguments that Huntington presents can be productively assessed in relation to another work, one with a very different vision, which appeared just two years before *Who Are We?* Richard Rodriguez's essay collection titled *Brown: The Last Discovery of America* is the last installment in a trilogy of his books.

While Huntington's book and Rodriguez's book are obviously quite different creatures, the first a political scientist's elaborations on immigration in the United States and the second a prose writer's essays on various aspects of cultural change, they can be read as unlikely participants in a dialogue that in the end turns on the persistence of memory and claims to define the vague and ominous concept of values. Moreover, we hear in Rodriguez and Huntington the distant echoes of the actors in the New World, Spain and England, whose interventions around the globe changed it forever. The juxtaposition of the two writers demonstrates that the culturological memory borne of the moment of settling and colonization frames two different representations of the same cultural space.

In *Brown*, Rodriguez continues to ponder questions he raised in his previous book, *Days of Obligation: An Argument with My Mexican Father* (1992). There, he reflected on the historical and cultural relationship between the two neighboring nations, the United States and Mexico, and on his own personal connection to that relationship. What does America have to say to that which falls outside the categories of black and white? Rodriguez recalls:

> I used to stare at the Indian in the mirror. The wide nostrils, the thick lips. Starring Paul Muni as Benito Juárez. Such a long face—such a long nose—sculpted by indifferent, blunt thumbs, and of such common clay. No one in my family had a face as dark or as Indian as mine. My face could not portray the ambition I brought to it. What could the United States of America say to me? I remember reading the ponderous conclusion of the Kerner Report in the sixties: two Americas, one white, one black—the prophecy of an eclipse too simple to account for the complexity of my face.[11]

Brown takes the tension emanating from the histories of colonization and racialism further and meditates on the idea of "brown" itself, on the implications of "brown" Mexico in relationship to "white" America, of "impurity" to "purity":

> Brown is the color most people in the United States associate with Latin America.
>
> Apart from stool sample, there is no browner smear in the Ameri-

> can imagination than the Rio Grande. No adjective has attached itself more often to the Mexican in America than "dirty"—which I assume gropes toward the simile "dirt-like," indicating dense concentration of melanin.[12]

"Brown," Rodriguez elaborates, is blending; it is the impure infusion of color, of sexuality, of history, of culture, of art—the infinite instances of entities brought into contact and spilling over into each other's spheres and spaces. It is confusion: "Brown forms at the border of contradiction."[13] It is also, by the same token, the impossibility of sustained purity. "Brown" is of course also the concrete physical category, and it spills over the southern border in the shape of thousands and thousands of brown bodies. They come not just as "unpleasant" reminders to some of that which is not pure; they also come with a perspective, a vision, and a route other than the English Protestant dissent that founded the United States.

Historically, the nation has always understood itself as an "east-to-west" country, with the settlers, colonists, and immigrants moving from coast to coast, from the proverbial "sea to shining sea." The frontier was interposed as one of the tropes for an emerging cultural self-understanding. But there was always a different perspective, a "south-to-north" or "north-to-south" perspective. This was embedded in the very anatomy of the geosocial landscape of what is today the American Southwest, long before the Puritans started ordering their universe around their self-appointed status as a beacon. On both sides of the present border, the legacies and memories of pre-Columbian civilizations, of Spanish colonialism and Mexican sovereignty, did not simply evaporate once Jefferson acquired the Louisiana Purchase, Austin delivered Texas, and Polk conquered half of Mexico. The place-names strewn across the American Southwest tell their own stories. "Brown," in other words, is code for a historical vector put into motion the moment Cortés set foot on Mexican land and asked for help in finding Moctezuma. Or it is code for the moment Columbus finally got Isabella's blessing to go west in order to rescue Spain from an alarming budget deficit and to confirm his conviction that there was land to the west. One could go further back; obviously, a point of original and absolute beginning is in one sense impossible to locate. From Rodriguez's perspective, however, physical and historical "brown" is biologically defined and situated in that particular moment when the Spaniard and the Indian met. From his apartment in downtown San Francisco he ponders along a south-to-north axis:

> Canada has never been much of an idea for Americans. We like Canada. Our good neighbor. Never hear them. Tidy.
>
> Downstairs . . . well, so many people come and go. What can they be up to? Mexico is a brown idea we would rather not discuss.[14]

However, this is precisely what Huntington wanted to discuss, and launching into a quest for national identity according to a route moving from East to West could only yield the kind of creedal concerns he voices. Moreover, this debate goes to the heart of the principles of dialogism that we find in Mikhail Bakhtin's concluding remarks in "Methodology for the Human Sciences." The following observation can meaningfully be brought to bear on the culturological context for both authors' positions:

> There is neither a first nor a last word and there are no limits to the dialogic context (it extends into the boundless past and the boundless future). Even *past* meanings, that is, those born in the dialogue of past centuries, can never be stable (finalized, ended once and for all)—they will always change (be renewed) in the process of subsequent, future development of the dialogue.
>
> At any moment in the development there are immense, boundless masses of forgotten contextual meanings, but at certain moments of the dialogue's subsequent development along the way they are recalled and invigorated in renewed form (in a new context). Nothing is absolutely dead: every meaning will have its homecoming festival. The problem of great time.[15]

American cultural and social history may be told as the sedimentation into a conglomerate of various culturological memories and their narratives, along with the "how"s and "when"s of their meanings' homecomings. As a nation of immigrants, the United States has long been moving away from purists' and essentialists' conceptions of one culture toward the manifestation of, and, in most cases, a recognition of the increasingly hybrid nature of the national character. In an optimistic view, this culturally conglomerated space perhaps even approximates Homi Bhabha's notion of third space, which

> bears the traces of those feelings and practises which inform it, just like a translation, so that hybridity puts together the traces of certain other meanings or discourses. It does not give them the authority of being prior in the sense of being original: they are prior only in the sense of being anterior. The process of cultural hybridity gives rise to something different, something new and unrecognisable, a new area of negotiation and representation.[16]

In this description, which echoes Bakhtin's comment on the reinvigoration of meanings in new contexts, hybridity constitutes a site of permanent unease and hence a site of permanent potential creativity. The skepticism about such processes can often be said to originate in and with what Andreas Huyssen calls the "turn toward memory," with the attendant desire to single out a separate space for what is perceived to be prior rather than anterior, originating rather than consecutive.[17] Bhabha's "traces of . . . feelings and practises" that potentially constitute new ground may thus take on a significance and rationale as paths back to safety and, as is often the case, as paths to a sense of and desire for purity, as Rodriguez reflects upon here: "Many Americans opt for a centrifugal view of the future, a black-and-white version—I don't mean skin but cultural intransigence—deduced from history as hatred. A future of real armies on opposing sides of a cultural divide—Muslims and Hindus, say."[18] Not only Americans are craving the neatness of such orderly separateness; that longing underlies currents that are stirring among all kinds of cultural practices and feelings. In 2009, for instance, Swiss voters said yes to a ban on the building of new minarets in their country, a decision that sent chills down the spines of a great many people everywhere. But the fact remained that the Swiss did not perceive minarets as acceptable participants in their social imaginary. We arrive here at the question of values, and the concept of values closes rather than opens up the flexibility of the magic that has driven and continues to drive the American social imaginary. In 2010, the Swiss decision is unthinkable in the United States. But that may change, and Huntington's call for creedal loyalties is a signal to that effect. It is perhaps nothing more than the inevitable outcome of vectors that have grown ever more involved and complex. Rodriguez reflects that:

> As lives meet, chafe, there will be a tendency to retreat. When the line between us is unenforced or seems to disappear, someone will surely be troubled and nostalgic for straight lines and will demand that the future give him the fundamental assurance of a border.
>
> A thought that haunts many African Americans I know is that they are the same distance from the slave owner as from the slave. Both strains have contributed to their bodies, to their waking spirits. I am the same distance from the conquistador as from the Indian. Righteousness should not come easily to any of us.[19]

These observations suggest the complexity and vastness of the perspective one has to have in regard to Huntington's arguments and warnings. Those warnings, it is important to note, arose precisely from the highly questionable claim to righteous origination. And yet Huntington's assessments of American social and cultural history are not wrong, nor are his deliberations on the gestalt of the American Creed incorrect. I would be the first to make my students read some of his chapters in this regard; they are rarely clear delineations of historical material that often becomes a set of confused and confusing overviews. The problem is rather that Huntington fails to name what he sees as the threat by its rightful name, and it is not "Mexicans" or "illegal aliens." It is the challenge of maintaining any cultural space free of the consequences of the influences—the feelings and practices—that that space sprang from, and is fostered by. The reaction to the threat of corruption is, by the same token, the desire to preserve certain routes and roots over and above certain others. There is nothing new or unusual about this, and American history has certainly had its share of similar concerns over similar trends, as Huntington's chapter "Emergence, Triumph, Erosion" indeed demonstrates. If we go back to the mid-nineteenth century, for instance, we find that John Calhoun, senator from South Carolina, articulated his doubts about the Mexican-American War and annexation thus: "Can we really incorporate a people so dissimilar to us in every respect," he asked, "so little qualified for free and popular government without certain destruction to our own political institutions?"[20] Lewis Cass, Calhoun's fellow senator, argued along similar lines, but whereas Calhoun urged the government to abandon the project, Cass was convinced that the undesirable population in the territories would simply dissolve: "We do not want the people of Mexico, either as citizens or subjects," he said. "All we want is a portion of territory, which they nominally hold, generally uninhabited, or, where at all, sparsely so, and with a population, which would soon recede, or identify itself with ours."[21] Many, many years later Rodriguez reflects, bemused:

> Standing in the burrito line in a Chinese neighborhood, I notice how many customers know the chopsticks of Spanish: "carnitas" and "guacamole" and "sí," "gracias," "refritos," and "caliente," and all the rest of what they need to know. And it occurs to me that the Chinese-American couple in front of me, by speaking Spanish, may actually be speaking American English.[22]

Rodriguez's "last discovery of America" is a kind of distorted mirror image of Huntington's realization, the discovery that Puritan purity browns, that creedal categories are not eternal, that worth and value are not permanent fissures. The discovery is perhaps also the discovery that the United States is not exempt from the legacies of its own imperialist and colonialist history: as in the case of European empires, Massey's social relations stretch out to form rims and spaces that are connected across time and across place.

A final question in relation to the "dialogue" I have staged here is, what prompted Huntington to voice his concerns at the time he did? Possible answers to that question are in large part related to his previous book. In *The Clash of Civilizations and the Remaking of World Order*, which appeared in 1996 and has since become standard reading for political scientists and others interested in global conflicts, Huntington presented and argued for a theory of global conflict, not between traditional nations, but between civilizations. "It is my hypothesis," he said,

> that the fundamental source of conflict in this new world will not be primarily ideological or primarily economic. The great divisions among humankind and the dominating source of conflict will be cultural. Nation states will remain the most powerful actors in world affairs, but the principal conflicts of global politics will occur between nations and groups of different civilizations. The clash of civilizations will dominate global politics.[23]

Culture, rather than ideological alliances, Huntington argued, increasingly provides the glue between nations. The broadest cultural entity is civilization, and the most important element that distinguishes one civilization from another is the spiritual or religious framework on which it is founded. Huntington identified seven or eight of these vast categories, among them the Islamic and the Western worlds. Edward Said, for one, was quick to argue against this interpretation of the world and its future. In "The Clash of Ignorance," he criticized Huntington for his utter disregard of the variations that exist within one culture, let alone within whole civilizations. His most poignant criticism, however, addressed the underlying conception of cultures as static historical entities: "Huntington is an ideologist, someone who wants to make 'civilizations' and 'identities' into what they are not: shut-down, sealed-off entities that have been purged of the myriad currents and countercurrents that animate human history."[24]

A similar oversight runs through *Who Are We?* As several commentators and critics have pointed out, the book essentially transfers to the national scene the rationales of global conflicts between civilizations, which are recast as conflicts between cultures and creeds. The salience of the creed is crucial in this respect, because, even if it cannot be strictly equated with a framework of spirituality and religiosity, it is close enough, as a cultural glue. A weakened faith in and commitment to the creed potentially means a weakened nation, a faltering project exposed. As a former advisor to the National Security Council, Huntington was acutely aware of the ways of history. "All societies," he says, "face recurring threats to their existence, to which they eventually succumb. Yet some societies, even when so threatened, are also capable of postponing their demise by halting and reversing the processes of decline and renewing their vitality and identity."[25]

This is curious wording, for if the idea of renewal is in effect the revitalization of the creed, then that seems to favor one route only, a return to Anglo-Protestant foundations and the universal embrace of the beliefs and ideas that those foundations stand for. This, however, has implications for the American imaginary. For if the magic or enchantment of the imaginary has always resided in and continues to reside in the universal allure of a particular kind of individualism and pursuit of advancement that exists within a religiously malleable framework and avoids specifications according to cultural and religious groupings, then a rerouting to specific cultural and ideological groundings could in fact threaten to disenchant the imaginary. I do not mean "disenchant" in the archaically religious or sacred sense in which Taylor employs the term, but in the sense of a desymbolizing direction that moves toward a hardening and limiting of the imaginary's magic range.

If we agree that the American imaginary, unlike its Western cousins, embeds its participants differently, in faith and commitment to the magic of what, as we shall see, Rodriguez calls the "quest of the 'I,'" then to channel the underpinnings for this into a specific origin may lead to an abstraction of its ground along the lines of Bakhtin's previously quoted warning about monologism: "Every cultural act lives essentially on the boundaries, and it derives its seriousness and significance from this fact. Separated by abstraction from these boundaries, it loses the ground of its being and becomes vacuous, arrogant, it degenerates and dies."[26] In the case of the American imaginary, these boundaries are constituted by what I referred to in the Introduction as the "vague contours of the definite certainties of identification," and their abstraction would be the hardening of these contours into ossified dislocation. It follows that both the imaginary and the founding documents would lose some of the universal appeal and attraction that they both constitute and are constituted by. The United States, in other words, would cease to be, as Deborah Madsen has put it, a "state of nation" and would become a "nation state," an (unexceptional) nation like most other nations.[27] But, if so, what would happen to America?

Futures of Enchantment

I end this chapter, and the book, with some reflections on something that Rodriguez says in an interview about views on America such as those refracted in Huntington's *Who Are We?*: "Everywhere in America now you see people who belong to various cultural traditions; the Anglo and the Hispanic are simply the two most obvious examples. The question for the future: Can a single life be more than one, can one know and behave according to several cultural influences?"[28] The most profound result of the juxtaposition of Rodriguez's and Huntington's statements is that the continuity and engagement of vectors pertaining to historical moments of colonialism and colonization continue to forge the United States as a nation and as a project of modernity. There are of course more than two vectors, and I have not even mentioned that which carries Native American cultural and political history, that which originates with and in the Middle Passage, or that which carries yet other encounters with the imaginary across the Pacific. The two I have dealt with are, as Rodriguez suggests, more conspicuous because they continue to collide and conflict over the same issues that originated in alternative geopolitical and cultural orientations in relation to the same shared space. In *Brown*, Rodriguez offers a more meditative contemplation of these movements: "North of the U.S.-Mexico border, brown appears as the color of the future. The adjective accelerates, becomes a verb: 'America is browning.' South of the border, brown sinks back into time. Brown is time."[29] Again, the acceleration has to do with the continued attraction and sway of the imaginary's promise, the multiple encounters with, the pursuits and interpretations of what it holds in store, stirred perhaps imperceptibly by the relentlessness of Bakhtin's meanings and their homecoming festivals. Condensing and complicating such movements is what Rodriguez calls the "quest of the 'I'" in relation to the future of America:

> I suspect that Huntington is most afraid of the loss of the individualistic culture that he calls America—the "I" civilization. The odd thing is that, at a time when American cultural influence is so widespread in the world, Huntington confesses to a fear that the United States will not be able to withstand the foreign. And the irony is that most of

> those immigrants coming to the United States, legally or illegally, are in quest of the "I," though they do not say it.[30]

If the American imaginary is indeed predicated on particular ideas of the obligation of advancement and individualism as socially beneficial, and on the inherent good of this singularly new project in the world, the continued salience of the imaginary's various institutions depends on the continued embrace of originating and underlying ideas and principles. Central to this embrace is the "quest of the 'I,'" but the exact institution of "I" will necessarily vary according to the traces of other imaginaries and their embeddedness in other times and places. In this conglomerate of pursuits, lived and remembered realities reach back to their heterogeneously constituted and instituted encounters with the master imaginary. The American social fabric may therefore be thought of as hosting a varied array of performances of "multiple modernities," but in the context of this "one" Western modernity, rather than the ones we so often think of as being somewhere else, as the so-called alternative modernities, as indeed Huntington did in *The Clash of Civilizations.*

We end these explorations and fieldtrips with a slightly different query, concerning the nature of institution itself (Latin *instituare*, from *in-* "in" + *statuere* "to establish, to cause to stand": how will the American imaginary uphold and accommodate its constituent parts? Paradoxically, the emphasis on creedal truths as signifying something very specific to specific groups contradicts the original promise and serves to disenchant the very bedrock on which the American imaginary is built. That would mean turning what Sacvan Bercovitch, in his discussion of the Winthrop variation, calls the "America game" into an endgame akin to its old world relatives, "identity to be resolved in three or four moves."[31] I doubt this was what Huntington intended, but his call for loyalty to specificities in effect undermines the very premises of what is to be rescued. The insistence on these premises is precisely what the film *Sugar*, with which I began in chapter 1, refracts, and its nuanced reflection on and of the American imaginary makes for an appropriate conclusion.

Most fundamentally, *Sugar* speaks to the ideal of the pursuit of individual aspiration. The scene at Roberto Clemente State Park, where the discarded players gather to play their own ball game, signifies as a field of dreams whose impact goes beyond the broken hopes of making it in baseball. The sequence of close-up shots becomes a testimony to something more, the multiple dreams of "I." The players, hailing from a range of Americas other than America, constitute the affirmation of the quest. They confirm the formation of cultural and economic rims that has been part of American history since its very beginnings. The possibilities extended to the individual and the hopes of their coming to fruition continue to attract and enchant J. Hector St. John de Crèvecoeur's *Americans-in-becoming*, for, as the last scenes in *Sugar* illustrate, in the end the "cold and broken hallelujah" is still praise. To many, this stubborn persistence in the worship of ideals and realities that statistics on poverty and unemployment reveal to be hopelessly flawed seems irrational at best. Given our knowledge of American social realities, it defies all logic. Yet there it is, all the faith and enchantedness of a continued "quest for the 'I,'" whatever that might come to mean. As with all magic, this is perhaps ultimately not to be subjected to the laws of rationality and logic; if it were, it would no longer enchant.

NOTES

Introduction

1. Robert Bellah, "Civil Religion in America," in *The Robert Bellah Reader*, ed. Robert N. Bellah and Steven M. Tipton (Durham, NC: Duke University Press, 2006), 233.

2. Sacvan Bercovitch, "A Model of Cultural Transvaluation: Puritanism, Modernity, and the New World Rhetoric" (paper presented at Early Modern Trans-Atlantic Encounters: England, Spain and the Americas, March 6–7, City University of New York), http://web.gc.cuny.edu/dept/renai/conf/Papers/Keynote/Bercovit.htm (accessed May 15, 2010).

3. I use the term "culturological" to emphasize an approach to culture that is diverse and dialogic, what Bakhtin called "organic unity" with the capacity of "transcending itself, that is, exceeding its own boundaries." See Mikhail Bakhtin, *Speech Genres and Other Late Essays*, ed. Michael Holquist and Caryl Emerson, trans. Vern W. McGee (Austin: University of Texas Press, 1986), 135. This has implications for methodology, in that the idea of culture remains descriptive rather than normative, multivalent rather than monovalent in its application. For a history and overview of the discipline of culturology, see Ellen N. Berry and Mikhail N. Epstein, *Transcultural Experiments: Russian and American Models of Creative Communication* (New York: St. Martin's Press, 1999).

4. Deborah Madsen, *American Exceptionalism* (Edinburgh: Edinburgh University Press, 1998), 1.

5. Winfried Fluck, "Theories of American Culture" (paper delivered at Transatlantic American Studies: Transcultural Vision of Identities in Images and Text, Humboldt University, Berlin, February 2005).

6. Djelal Kadir, "Introduction: America and Its Studies," *PMLA* 118, no. 1 (2003): 10.

7. Fluck, "Theories," 3.

8. Richard Rodriguez, *Brown: The Last Discovery of America* (New York: Viking, 2002), 161.

9. Arif Dirlik, "American Studies in the Time of Empire," *Comparative American Studies* 2, no. 3 (2004): 288.

10. Orm Øverland, introduction to *A Saloonkeeper's Daughter*, by Drude Krog Janson, ed. Orm Øverland, trans. Gerald Thorson (Baltimore: Johns Hopkins University Press, 2002), xi–xii.

11. Raymond Geuss, "Kultur, Bildung, Geist," *History and Theory* 35, no. 2 (1996): 151–64, footnote 154.

12. Jeffrey Sammons, "The Bildungsroman for Nonspecialists: An Attempt at a Clarification," in *Reflection and Action: Essays on the Bildungsroman*, ed. James Hardin (Columbia: University of South Carolina Press, 1991), 29.

13. Charles Taylor, *Modern Social Imaginaries* (Durham, NC: Duke University Press, 2002), 23.

14. Cornelius Castoriadis, *Figures of the Thinkable*, trans. Helen Arnold (Stanford, CA: Stanford University Press, 2007), 100.

15. Robert Beuka, *SuburbiaNation* (New York: Macmillan Palgrave, 2004), 4.

16. Vladimir Nabokov, *Pnin* (London: Heinemann, 1957), 20.

17. Doreen B. Massey, *Space, Place, and Gender* (Cambridge: Polity, 1994), 2.

18. Guillermo Gómez-Peña, *Ethno-Techno: Writings on Performance, Activism, and Pedagogy* (London: Taylor and Francis, 2005), 16.

Chapter 1: The Imaginary

1. *Sugar*, motion picture, directed by Anna Boden and Ryan Fleck (New York: JourneyMan Pictures, 2008).

2. Andrew O'Hehir, "Sugar: Best Baseball Movie Ever," review of *Sugar*, directed by Anna Boden and Ryan Fleck, *Salon*, April 3, 2009, http://www.salon.com/ent/movies/btm/feature/2009/04/03/sugar/index.html (accessed May 30, 2009).

3. Ibid.

4. Roberto González Echevarría, quoted in Dave Zirin, "Say It Ain't So, Big Leagues," *Nation*, October 26, 2005, 2.

5. For a brilliant representation of the public perception of Latinos as all the same and as all Mexicans, see Sergio Arau's film, *A Day Without a Mexican* (2004).

6. Zirin, "Say It Ain't So," 1.

7. David Chidester, quoted in Thomas F. Dailey, "Believing in Baseball: the Religious Power of Our National Pastime," *Logos* 6, no. 2 (2003): 66.

8. Charles Taylor, *Modern Social Imaginaries* (Durham, NC: Duke University Press, 2002), 23.

9. Cornelius Castoriadis, *The Imaginary Institution of Society* (Cambridge, MA: MIT Press, 1987), 3.

10. Cornelius Castoriadis, *Figures of the Thinkable*, trans. Helen Arnold (Stanford, CA: Stanford University Press, 2007), 205.

11. Ibid.

12. Ibid., 71.

13. Mikhail Bakhtin, *Art and Answerability: Early Philosophical Essays*, ed. Michael Holquist and Vadim Liapunov, trans. Vadim Liapunov (Austin: University of Texas Press, 1990), 274.

14. Sacvan Bercovitch, "Games of Chess: A Model of Literary and Cultural Studies," in *Centuries' Ends, Narrative Means*, ed. Robert Newman (Stanford, CA: Stanford University Press, 1996), 54–55.

15. Castoriadis, *Figures of the Thinkable*, 127.

16. Castoriadis, *Imaginary Institution*, 128.

17. Taylor, *Modern Social Imaginaries*, 23.

18. Ibid., 3–4.

19. Ibid., 21–22.

20. Ibid., 49.

21. Castoriadis, *Imaginary Institution*, 161, 156.

22. Charles Taylor, "Buffered and Porous Selves," comment on *The Secular Age*, *The Immanent Frame*, posted September 2, 2008, http://www.ssrc.org/blogs/immanent_frame/ (accessed March 2, 2009).

23. Taylor, *Modern Social Imaginaries*, 176.

24. Djelal Kadir, quoted in Sophia A. McClennen, "Inter-American Studies or Imperial American Studies?" *Comparative American Studies* 3, no. 4 (2005): 397.

25. "The Life Story of a Lithuanian," in *The Life Stories of Undistinguished Americans as Told by Themselves*, ed. Hamilton Holt (1906; New York/London: Routledge, 2000), 10.

26. Taylor, *Modern Social Imaginaries*, 151.

27. Ibid.

28. Walter D. Mignolo and Freya Schiwy, "Beyond Dichotomies: Translation/Transculturation and the Colonial Difference," in *Beyond Dichotomies: Histories, Identities, Cultures, and the Challenge of Globalization*, ed. Elisabeth Mudimbe-Boyi (New York: SUNY Press, 2002), 266.

29. Bronislaw Malinowski, quoted in Mauricio Augusto Font, Alfonso W. Quiroz, and Pamela Maria Smorkaloff, "Introduction. The Intellectual Legacy of Fernando Ortiz," in *Cuban Counterpoints: The Legacy of Fernando Ortiz*, ed. Mauricio A. Font and Alfonso W. Quiroz (Lanham, MD: Lexington Books, 2005), xvi.

30. Doreen B. Massey, *Space, Place, and Gender* (Cambridge: Polity, 1994), 2.

Chapter 2: "Perpetual Progress" in Drude Krog Janson's A Saloonkeeper's Daughter

1. The book was also published in Copenhagen at roughly the same time, but the publisher there did not care for the American-sounding title. The novel came out as *En Ung Pike* [A young girl].

2. Orm Øverland, introduction to *A Saloonkeeper's Daughter*, by Drude Krog Janson, ed. Orm Øverland, trans. Gerald Thorson (Baltimore: Johns Hopkins University Press, 2002); xi–xxxiv, xi.

3. The diversity of approaches is evident in the range of topics covered in Asbjørn Grønstad and Lene Johannessen, eds., *To Become the Self One Is: A Critical Companion to "A Saloonkeeper's Daughter"* (Oslo: Novus Press, 2005).

4. For a detailed discussion of religion in Janson's novel, see Øyvind Gulliksen, "The Lutheran Immigrant Turns Unitarian: Bjørnstjerne Bjørnson, William Ellery Channing, and Religious Idealism in *A Saloonkeeper's Daughter*," in Grønstad and Johannessen, *To Become the Self*, 15–30.

5. For a comparative discussion of women's liberation movements and the relationship between European and American writings of the period, see Anne Holden Rønning, "*A Saloonkeeper's Daughter* and the Woman Question," in Grønstad and Johannessen, *To Become the Self*, 31–42. In a similar vein Fredrik Brøgger argues that, in her depiction of Astrid's plight, Janson's representation ties directly into "the women's rights debate of the 1870s and 80s in America and Scandinavia," echoing the acclaimed Norwegian author Camilla Collett ("'Good Lord, They're All the Same': Nature and Sexuality in Drude Krog Janson's *A Saloonkeeper's Daughter*," in Grønstad and Johannessen, *To Become the Self*, 142).

6. Ken Luebbering, "Redefining 'American': The Creation of Identity in *A Saloonkeeper's Daughter*," in Grønstad and Johannessen, *To Become the Self*; 57–66, 58.

7. Gerald Thorson, translator's preface to *A Saloonkeeper's Daughter*, x.

8. Øverland, introduction to *A Saloonkeeper's Daughter*; xi, xi–xii. The phrase takes its cue from the work of the Longfellow Institute on the multilingual nature of American literature (Werner Sollors and March Shells). *A Saloonkeeper's Daughter* was published as the first novel in the Institute Series.

9. Drude Krog Janson, *A Saloonkeeper's Daughter*, ed. Orm Øverland, trans. Gerald Thorson (Baltimore: Johns Hopkins University Press, 2002), 23.

10. J. Hector St. John de Crèvecoeur, "Letter III. What is an American?" in *Letters from an American Farmer*, ed. William Peterfield Trent (New York: Fox, Duffield and Company, 1904), 55.

11. Charles Taylor, *Modern Social Imaginaries* (Durham, NC: Duke University Press, 2002), 3.

12. Ibid., 4.

13. Ibid., 151.

14. Franco Moretti, *The Way of the World: The Bildungsroman in European Culture* (London: Verso, 1987), 227.

15. Jeffrey Sammons, "The Bildungsroman for Nonspecialists: An Attempt at a Clarification," in *Reflection and Action: Essays on the Bildungsroman*, ed. James Hardin (Columbia: University of South Carolina Press, 1991), 29.

16. Richard Koselleck, *The Practice of Conceptual History: Timing History, Spacing Concepts* (Stanford, CA: Stanford University Press, 2002), 174.

17. Janson, *Saloonkeeper's Daughter*; 19, 20.

18. Ibid., 31.

19. Ibid., 32.

20. The author Bjørnstjerne Bjørnson (1832–1910) was a major public figure in

Norwegian as well as international cultural and political life in the latter half of the nineteenth century. He was awarded the Nobel Prize for Literature in 1903. Bjørnson was a close friend of Drude Krog Janson and her husband, and he toured the Midwest in 1880–81 to give lectures in immigrant communities. For a more comprehensive treatment, see Øverland, introduction to *A Saloonkeeper's Daughter*.

21. Ibid., 73.

22. Moretti, *Way of the World*, 45.

23. Janson, *Saloonkeeper's Daughter*, 97.

24. Walter Sokel, "The Blackening of the Breast: The Narrative of Existential Education and R. M. Rilke's *The Notebooks of Malte Brigge*," in Hardin, *Reflection and Action*, 332.

25. Moretti, *Way of the World*, 23.

26. Janson, *Saloonkeeper's Daughter*, 99.

27. Ibid.; 103, 104.

28. Ibid., 119.

29. Gulliksen, "The Lutheran Immigrant Turns Unitarian," in Grønstad and Johannessen, *To Become the Self*, 27.

30. Ibid., 120.

31. Mikhail Bakhtin, *Problems of Dostoevsky's Poetics* (Manchester, UK: Manchester University Press, 1984), 106.

32. Janson, *Saloonkeeper's Daughter*, 132.

33. Ibid., 134.

34. Ibid., 136.

35. Axel Nissen, "*A Saloonkeeper's Daughter* in the Company of Women," in Grønstad and Johannessen, *To Become the Self*; 115, 122. Nissen in fact concludes his discussion of the novel by suggesting that it is "arguably the first lesbian novel in American literature" (127).

36. Taylor, *Modern Social Imaginaries*, 25.

37. Sacvan Bercovitch, "Games of Chess: A Model of Literary and Cultural Studies," in *Centuries' Ends, Narrative Means*, ed. Robert Newman (Stanford, CA: Stanford University Press, 1996), 33.

38. Janson, *Saloonkeeper's Daughter*, 143.

39. Ibid.; 150, 147.

40. Bercovitch, "Games of Chess," in Newman, *Centuries' Ends*, 54.

41. David Lowenthal, *The Past Is a Foreign Country* (Cambridge: Cambridge University Press, 1990), 105.

42. Janson, *Saloonkeeper's Daughter*; 145, 149.

Chapter 3: Songs of Different Selves: Whitman and Gonzales

1. Benjamin R. Barber, "Walt Whitman's Song of Democracy," in *Walt Whitman: Where the Future Becomes Present*, ed. David Haven Blake and Michael Robertson (Iowa City: University of Iowa Press, 2008), 91.

2. Cornelius Castoriadis, *The Imaginary Institution of Society* (Cambridge, MA: MIT Press, 1987), 3.

3. Cornelius Castoriadis, *Figures of the Thinkable*, trans. Helen Arnold (Stanford, CA: Stanford University Press, 2007); 95, 100.

4. Kirsten Gruesz, "Walt Whitman, Latino Poet," in Blake and Robertson, *Walt Whitman*, 152.

5. Walt Whitman, "Song of Myself," in *Leaves of Grass* ("Death-Bed Edition"), introduced by William Carlos Williams (New York: Modern Library, 2000); Sections 24, 64. All subsequent references to "Song of Myself" are to this edition.

6. Walt Whitman, "Starting from Paumanok," in *Walt Whitman: Complete Poetry and Collected Prose*, ed. Justin Kaplan (New York: Library of America, 1982), 183.

7. Ibid.; Sections 33, 76–86, 34, 86. The poet writes: "(I tell not the fall of Alamo, / Not one escaped to tell the fall of Alamo, / The hundred and fifty are dumb yet at Alamo.)"

8. Walt Whitman, "Shall We Fight It Out?" *Brooklyn Daily Eagle*, May 11, 1846, Brooklyn Public Library, http://eagle.brooklynpubliclibrary.org/Default/Skins/BEagle/Client.asp?Skin=BEagle (accessed May 20, 2010).

9. Walt Whitman, "One's-Self I Sing," in *Leaves of Grass*, 1.

10. Castoriadis, *Imaginary Institution*, 3.

11. Charles Taylor, *Modern Social Imaginaries* (Durham, NC: Duke University Press, 2002); 3, 15.

12. Ibid., 153.

13. Ralph Waldo Emerson, "The Transcendentalist," in *The Collected Works of Ralph Waldo Emerson, Volume I: Nature, Addresses, and Lectures*, ed. Alfred R. Ferguson, introduction by Robert E. Spiller (Cambridge, MA: Belknap Press of Harvard University Press, 1971), 201.

14. Whitman, "Song of Myself," Section 2, in *Leaves of Grass*.

15. Ralph Waldo Emerson, "The Poet," in *The Collected Works of Ralph Waldo Emerson, Volume III: Essays: Second Series*, ed. Alfred R. Ferguson and Jean Ferguson Carr, introduction by Joseph Slater (Cambridge, MA: Belknap Press of Harvard University Press, 1983); 3–24, 21–22.

16. Whitman, "Song of Myself," Sections 15, 54; in *Leaves of Grass*.

17. Castoriadis, *Imaginary Institution*, 3.

18. Taylor, *Modern Social Imaginaries*, 175.

19. Whitman, "Song of Myself," Sections 23, 63; in *Leaves of Grass*.

20. Sacvan Bercovitch, "Games of Chess: A Model of Literary and Cultural Studies," in *Centuries' Ends, Narrative Means*, ed. Robert Newman (Stanford, CA: Stanford University Press, 1996), 33–34.

21. Taylor, *Modern Social Imaginaries*, 176.

22. Ibid., 151.

23. Ramón Saldívar, *Chicano Narrative: The Dialectics of Difference* (Madison: University of Wisconsin Press, 1990), 13.

24. Rodolfo Gonzales, *I am Joaquín*, 3rd ed. (New York: Bantam Books, 1975), 6–9.

25. Ibid., 51.

26. Whitman, "Song of Myself," Sections 1, 33; in *Leaves of Grass.*

27. Matt Meier and Feliciano Ribera, *Mexican Americans/American Mexicans: From Conquistadors to Chicanos* (New York: Hill and Wang, 1995), 75.

28. Juan Bruce-Novoa, *Retro-Space: Collected Essays on Chicano Literature* (Houston: Arte Público Press, 1990), 103.

29. Gonzales, *I am Joaquín*, 19.

30. Ibid., 40–42.

31. Doreen Massey, *For Space* (London: Sage Publications, 2005), 9.

32. Mieke Bal, "Heterochrony in the Act: The Migratory Politics of Time" (paper presented at the conference Encuentro II Migratory Politics of the Migratory, Amsterdam, Holland, September 19–21, 2007, http://home.medewerker.uva.nl/m.g.bal/page3.html [accessed May 21, 2010]).

33. Gonzales, *I am Joaquín*, 98.

34. Whitman, "Song of Myself," Sections 1, 33; in *Leaves of Grass.*

35. Langston Hughes, "I, Too," in *The Collected Poems of Langston Hughes*, ed. A. Rampersad (New York: Vintage, 1995), 46.

36. Gonzales, *I am Joaquín*, 98.

37. Whitman, "Song of Myself," sections 24, 65, 23, 63; in *Leaves of Grass.*

38. José E. Limón, *Mexican Ballads, Chicano Poems: History and Influence in Mexican-American Social Poetry* (Berkeley: University of California Press, 1992), 18–20.

39. Saldívar, *Chicano Narrative*, 35.

40. Américo Paredes, "*With His Pistol in His Hand*": *A Border Ballad and Its Hero* (Austin: University of Texas Press, 1990).

41. Richard Bauman, introduction to *Folklore and Culture on the Texas-Mexican Border*, by Américo Paredes, ed. Richard Bauman (Austin: CMAS Books, 1993), xiv.

42. Since the 1970s a whole new subtype of *corrido* has emerged, the *narcocorrido*, chronicling and singing the merits of drug barons and drug trafficking on the border.

43. To this day, the production is widely watched and used in college and high school classes, and as of the summer of 2010 it may be viewed at: http://www.youtube.com/watch?v=U6M6qOG2O-o.

44. Mikhail Bakhtin, *Speech Genres and Other Late Essays*, ed. Michael Holquist and Caryl Emerson, trans. Vern W. McGee (Austin: University of Texas Press, 1986), 5.

45. Hayden White, "Good of Their Kind," *New Literary History* 34 (2003): 367.

46. The *corrido* shares this feature with numerous oral traditions around the world, in which the most important element is often that the poet or singer cannot speak until allowed to do so by the audience or community.

47. Gonzales, *I am Joaquín*, 10–12.

48. Orm Øverland, *Immigrant Minds, American Identities: Making the United States Home, 1870–1930* (Urbana and Chicago: University of Illinois Press, 2000), 8.

49. Ibid., 88.

50. Massey, *For Space*; 6, 5.

51. Gonzales, *I am Joaquín*, 52.

52. Doreen B. Massey, *Space, Place, and Gender* (Cambridge: Polity, 1994), 2.

Chapter 4: The "Long Empty Moment": Richard Ford's The Sportswriter

1. Charles Taylor, *Modern Social Imaginaries* (Durham, NC: Duke University Press, 2002), 194.

2. Cornelius Castoriadis, *The Imaginary Institution of Society* (Cambridge, MA: MIT Press, 1987), 161.

3. Richard Ford, *The Sportswriter* (London: Vintage, 2003), 9. All subsequent page references are to this edition.

4. Lewis Mumford, *The City in History: Its Origins, Its Transformations, and Its Prospects* (New York: Harcourt, Brace and World, 1961), 553.

5. Philip Y. Nicholson, "The Elusive Soul of the Suburbs: An Inquiry into Contemporary Political Culture," in *Suburbia Re-examined*, ed. Barbara M. Kelly (New York: Greenwood Press, 1989), 207.

6. Robert Beuka, *SuburbiaNation* (New York: Macmillan Palgrave, 2004), 21.

7. Paul Knox, "Vulgaria: The Re-Enchantment of Suburbia," *Opolis: An International Journal of Suburban and Metropolitan Studies* 1, no. 2 (2005): 4, http://repositories.cdlib.org/cssd/opolis/vol1/iss2/art3 (accessed May 26, 2009).

8. Michel Foucault, "Of Other Spaces," in *Heterotopia and the City: Public Space in a Postcivil Society*, ed. Lieven de Cauter and Michiel Dehane (London: Routledge, 2008); 17, 21.

9. "Becoming a Levittowner: Community Life," *Saturday Evening Post*, 1954, in "Levittown, Pa.: Building the American Dream," State Museum of Pennsylvania, 2003, http://web1.fandm.edu/levittown/default.html (accessed May 15, 2010).

10. Cornelius Castoriadis, *Figures of the Thinkable*, trans. Helen Arnold (Stanford, CA: Stanford University Press, 2007), 100.

11. Ford, *Sportswriter*, 30.

12. Reinhold Görling, "Topology of Borders in Turkish-German Cinema," in *Border Poetics De-limited*, ed. Johan Schimanski and Stephen Wolfe (Hannover: Wehrhahn Verlag, 2004), 149.

13. Ford, *Sportswriter*, 12.

14. Ibid.; 45, 56.

15. Beuka, *SuburbiaNation*, 25.

16. Ford, *Sportswriter*, 201–2.

17. Ibid., 49.

18. Ibid., 10.

19. Fred Hobson, "*The Sportswriter*: Post-Faulkner, Post-Southern?" in *Perspectives on Richard Ford*, ed. Huey Guagliardo (Jackson: University Press of Mississippi, 2000), 93.

20. Edward Dupuey, "The Confessions of an Ex-Suicide: Relenting and Recovering in Richard Ford's *The Sportswriter*," in Guagliardo, *Perspectives on Richard Ford*, 72.

21. Ford, *Sportswriter*; 16, 48, 16, 86.

22. Hobson, "*The Sportswriter*," in Guagliardo, *Perspectives on Richard Ford*, 87.

23. Bill Owens, *Suburbia* (San Francisco: Straight Arrow Books, 1972).

24. Hobson, "*The Sportswriter*," in Guagliardo, *Perspectives on Richard Ford*, 90.

25. Ford, *The Sportswriter*, 136.

26. Ibid.; 121, 170.

27. Ibid.; 201, 344, 346.

28. Ibid., 371.

29. Ibid., 377.

30. Ibid., 381.

31. David Lodge, *The Modes of Modern Writing: Metaphor, Metonymy, and the Typology of Modern Literature* (London: E. Arnold, 1977), 99.

32. Mikhail Bakhtin, *Art and Answerability: Early Philosophical Essays*, ed. Michael Holquist and Vadim Liapunov, trans. Vadim Liapunov (Austin: University of Texas Press, 1990), 209.

33. Jacques Lacan, *Ecrits: A Selection*, ed. Bruce Fink and Heloise Fink, trans. Russell Grigg (New York: W. W. Norton and Company, 2004), 158.

34. Ford, *Sportswriter*, 381.

35. Gilles Deleuze, *Francis Bacon: The Logic of Sensation* (London and New York: Continuum, 2003), 1–2.

Chapter 5: "Relations Stretched Out" in the American Imaginary

1. Doreen Massey, *For Space* (London: Sage Publications, 2005), 9.

2. Ana Menéndez, *In Cuba I Was a German Shepherd* (New York: Grove Press, 2001). All references are to this edition. As the daughter of Cuban exiles, Ana Menéndez would seem to fall into the category of intellectuals and writers called Cuban-American ethnic writers. In *Cuban-American Literature of Exile*, Isabel Alvarez Borland distinguishes between this category and the one she labels "the one and a half" generation. The latter consists of writers who were born in Cuba and came to the United States as adolescents. I am not entirely sure that such categories are helpful. For when a writer such as Menéndez writes out of a community, as she clearly does, we need to look at the defining circumstances of that community. And while communities naturally change

over time, the Cuban-American community is still very close to its exilic origins. The ideational power of originating moments of creation (of the individual or of the community) must not be overlooked. So while Menéndez may fit Borland's category of the Cuban-American ethnic writer, she demonstrates an awareness of and sensitivity to the condition of exile that suggests she is aesthetically and ideationally closer to the generation before her. While categories like these are of no consequence in and of themselves, the circumstance of exile does figure crucially in *In Cuba I Was a German Shepherd*, a work far removed from the events of 1959.

3. Cornelius Castoriadis, *The Imaginary Institution of Society* (Cambridge, MA: MIT Press, 1987), 3.

4. Norma Klahn, "Chicana and Mexicana Feminist Practices: De/Linking Cultural Imaginaries," in *Genealogies of Displacement: Diaspora/Exile/Migration and Chicana/o/Latina/o/Latin American/Peninsular Literary and Cultural Studies*, ed. Jordi Aladro, Norma Klahn, Lourdes Martínez-Echazábal, and Juan Poblete, *Nuevo Texto Critico* 29/32 (2002–3), 168.

5. Charles Taylor, *Modern Social Imaginaries* (Durham, NC: Duke University Press, 2002), 23.

6. Mieke Bal, "Heterochrony in the Act: The Migratory Politics of Time" (paper presented at the conference Encuentro II Migratory Politics of the Migratory, Amsterdam, Holland, September 19–21, 2007, http://home.medewerker.uva.nl/m.g.bal/page3.html [accessed May 21, 2010]).

7. Dianne Oenning Thompson, *The Brothers Karamazov and the Poetics of Memory* (Cambridge: Cambridge University Press, 1991), 3.

8. Menéndez, *In Cuba*, 3.

9. Ibid., 9.

10. Ibid., 11.

11. Michael Seidel, *Exile and the Narrative Imagination* (New Haven, CT: Yale University Press, 1986), 2.

12. Hayden White, *Tropics of Discourse: Essays in Cultural Criticism* (Baltimore: Johns Hopkins University Press, 1978), 5.

13. Antonio Barcelona, "The Cognitive Theory of Metaphor and Metonymy," in *Metaphor and Metonymy at the Crossroads: A Cognitive Perspective*, ed. A. Barcelona (Berlin and New York: Mouton de Gruyter, 2000), 3–4.

14. Hayden White, *Metahistory: The Historical Imagination in Nineteenth-Century Europe* (Baltimore: Johns Hopkins University Press, 1975), 33.

15. Barcelona, "Theory of Metaphor and Metonymy," in Barcelona, *Metaphor and Metonymy*, 2.

16. Cornelius Castoriadis, *Figures of the Thinkable*, trans. Helen Arnold (Stanford, CA: Stanford University Press, 2007), 205.

17. Menéndez, *In Cuba*, 24.

18. A type of men's shirt that originated in eighteenth-century Cuba and spread to other parts of the Americas by way of Yucatán, Mexico, where wealthy Cubans often vacationed.

19. Menéndez, *In Cuba*, 25.

20. Ibid., 26.

21. Seidel, *Exile*, 11. Emphasis mine.

22. Barcelona, "Theory of Metaphor and Metonymy," in Barcelona, *Metaphor and Metonymy*, 4.

23. For a seminal discussion of this, see Roman Jacobson, "Two Aspects of Language and Two Types of Aphasic Disturbances," in *Fundamentals of Language*, ed. Roman Jacobson and Morris Halle (The Hague: Mouton, 1971), 49–70.

24. See Michael Ugarte, *Shifting Ground: Spanish Civil War Exile Literature* (Durham, NC: Duke University Press, 1989).

25. Ibid., 22.

26. Menéndez, *In Cuba*; 41, 34.

27. Ibid., 327.

28. Ibid., 7.

29. Gerard Genette, *Figures of Literary Discourse*, trans. Alan Sheridan, introduction by Marie-Rose Logan (New York: Columbia University Press, 1982), 47.

30. White, *Tropics of Discourse*, 2.

31. Genette, *Figures of Literary Discourse*, 47.

32. Roland Barthes, *A Lover's Discourse: Fragments*, trans. Richard Howard (New York: Hill and Wang, 2000), 6.

33. Menéndez, *In Cuba*, 9.

34. "Manicero" means "peanut vendor." It is also the name of a famous Cuban *son* hit of the 1930s, as well as a type of dance.

35. Menéndez, *In Cuba*, 10.

36. Jacobson, "Two Aspects of Language," in Jacobson and Halle, *Fundamentals of Language*, 67.

37. Seidel, *Exile*, ix.

38. Menéndez, *In Cuba*, 51.

39. Ibid., 72.

40. Roland Barthes, *Camera Lucida. Reflections on Photography*, trans. Richard Howard (New York: Hill and Wang, 2000), 4.

41. Menéndez, *In Cuba*; 59, 73.

42. One may object, and rightfully so, that the impulse to replicate pagan decor in Christian edifices was originally marked by the desire to conserve a "piece of the past." We see, however, an incorporation that quickly morphs into metaphorical expression, and herein resides the difference between the examples of metaphorical and metonymic manifestations that I discuss.

43. Cecilie Stang, quoted in Siv Ringdal, *Det Amerikanske Lista: Med 110 Volt i Huset* [The American Lista: With 110 volts at home] (Oslo: Pax, 2002), 55. Translation mine. The title refers to the longstanding custom of bringing back electrical appliances from the United States.

44. These are all names of various places and regions in other parts of Norway. *Bygd* means "township, village."

45. Ånen Årli, *Kvinesdal: Ei bygdebok* [Kvinesdal: A local history], Vol. 3 (Flekkefjord: Hegland Boktrykkeri, 1972), 311. Translation mine.

46. Oswald I. Gilbertson, *Sånn va dæ då i Kvinesdal: Som æg minnest dæ . . .* [The way it was then in Kvinesdal: As I recall it . . .] (Oswald Gilbertson, 1998), 155. Translation mine.

47. Ove-Kjell Ryerson, manager, *USA Experten*, Kvinesdal, e-mail message to author, June 6, 2002.

48. Steinar Egeland, "Festschrift," (Kvinesdal: Steinar Egeland, 1992), 8. Translation mine.

49. Gilbertson, *Sånn va dæ då*, 156.

50. Castoriadis, *Figures of the Thinkable*, 127.

51. Terence Turner, quoted in Phyllis Perrin Wilcox, *Metaphor in American Sign Language* (Washington, D.C.: Gallaudet University Press, 2000), 18.

52. Sacvan Bercovitch, "Games of Chess: A Model of Literary and Cultural Studies," in *Centuries' Ends, Narrative Means*, ed. Robert Newman (Stanford, CA: Stanford University Press, 1996), 54.

Chapter 6: Recalling America: Huntington and Rodriguez

1. Samuel Huntington, *Who Are We? The Challenges to America's Identity* (New York: Simon and Schuster, 2004), 9.

2. Ibid., xvi.

3. Ibid., 30.

4. Samuel Huntington, "The Special Case of Mexican Immigration," *The American Enterprise Online* 11 (December 2000): 20–22, 22.

5. Samuel Huntington, "The Hispanic Challenge," *Foreign Policy* (March/April 2004): 30–45. Available at: http://www.foreignpolicy.com/articles/2004/03/01/the_hispanic_challenge.

6. These are the titles of the subsections in "The Hispanic Challenge," but the focus on how Hispanic immigrants in general and Mexican immigrants in particular differ from other groups remains constant in *Who Are We?* as well. This, in addition to the prepublication of this article, which in the book was to be chapter 9, "Mexican Immigration and Hispanization," suggests that immigration from south of the border was a main point on the agenda that Huntington set up.

7. Huntington, "Hispanic Challenge," 1. Unlike other "new immigrants," Latinos, and especially Mexicans, are able to sustain ties to their mother country and forge cultural continuity in a way no other group historically has been able to do. There is no doubt that major demographic shifts are taking place. What Huntington does not mention, however, is that a great many earlier immigrant groups have followed the same pattern, starting out as cultural and linguistic enclaves, and, as generations have passed, transitioning into so-called mainstream society. (In the nineteenth century, the Irish, Italians, and even Scandinavians exemplified this.)

8. Louis Menand, "Patriot Games: The New Nativism of Samuel P. Huntington," *The New Yorker*, May 17, 2004 (accessed September 2, 2004).

9. Alan Wolfe, "Native Son: Samuel Huntington Defends the Homeland," review essay, *Foreign Affairs*, May/June 2004 (accessed September 4, 2004).

10. Daniel Lazare, "Diversity and Its Discontents," *The Nation*, May 27, 2004, 3 (accessed September 4, 2004).

11. Richard Rodriguez, *Days of Obligation: An Argument with My Mexican Father* (New York: Viking, 1992), 1.

12. Richard Rodriguez, *Brown: The Last Discovery of America* (New York: Viking, 2002), xii.

13. Ibid., xi.

14. Ibid., 161.

15. Mikhail Bakhtin, *Speech Genres and Other Late Essays*, ed. Michael Holquist and Caryl Emerson, trans. Vern W. McGee (Austin: University of Texas Press, 1986), 170.

16. Homi Bhabha, "The Third Space: Interview with Homi Bhabha," in *Identity, Community, Culture, Difference*, ed. J. Rutherford (London: Lawrence and Wishart, 1990), 211.

17. Andreas Huyssen, "Present Pasts: Media, Politics, Amnesia," in *Globalization*, ed. A. Appadurai (Durham, NC: Duke University Press, 2001), 65.

18. Rodriguez, *Brown*, 225.

19. Ibid., 227–28.

20. Quoted in Reginald Horsman, *Race and Manifest Destiny: The Origins of American Racial Anglo-Saxonism* (Cambridge, MA: Harvard University Press, 1981), 241.

21. Quoted in David G. Gutiérrez, *Walls and Mirrors: Mexican Americans, Mexican Immigrants, and the Politics of Ethnicity* (Berkeley: University of California Press, 1995), 16.

22. Rodriguez, *Brown*, 11.

23. Samuel Huntington, *The Clash of Civilizations and the Remaking of World Order* (New York: Simon and Schuster, 1996), 1.

24. Edward Said, "The Clash of Ignorance," *The Nation*, October 22, 2001.

25. Huntington, *Who Are We?* xvii.

26. Mikhail Bakhtin, *Art and Answerability: Early Philosophical Essays*, ed. Michael Holquist and Vadim Liapunov, trans. Vadim Liapunov (Austin: University of Texas Press, 1990), 274.

27. Deborah Madsen, "Keynote Lecture" (paper presented at the Salzburg Global Seminar, Transnationalism and Immigration Shock in American Society and Literature, Salzburg, Austria, October 30–November 2, 2008).

28. Richard Rodriguez, interview in Lene Johannessen, "Amerikas Historier På Langs," [America's stories: Perpendicular], *Replikk* 26 (Bergen: Havel, 2008), 20. The quotations in this text are from the original interview.

29. Rodriguez, *Brown*, xii.

30. Rodriguez, "Amerikas Historier På Langs," 20.

31. Sacvan Bercovitch, "Games of Chess: A Model of Literary and Cultural Studies," in *Centuries' Ends, Narrative Means*, ed. Robert Newman (Stanford, CA: Stanford University Press, 1996), 54.

BIBLIOGRAPHY

Bakhtin, Mikhail. *Art and Answerability: Early Philosophical Essays.* Edited by Michael Holquist and Vadim Liapunov. Translated by Vadim Liapunov. Austin: University of Texas Press, 1990.

———. *Problems of Dostoevsky's Poetics.* Manchester, UK: Manchester University Press, 1984.

———. *Speech Genres and Other Late Essays.* Edited by Michael Holquist and Caryl Emerson. Translated by Vern W. McGee. Austin: University of Texas Press, 1986.

Bal, Mieke. "Heterochrony in the Act: The Migratory Politics of Time." Paper presented at the conference Encuentro II Migratory Politics of the Migratory, Amsterdam, Holland, September 19–21, 2007.

Barber, Benjamin R. "Walt Whitman's Song of Democracy." In Blake and Robertson, *Walt Whitman*, 91–105. Iowa City: University of Iowa Press, 2008.

Barcelona, Antonio. "The Cognitive Theory of Metaphor and Metonymy." In *Metaphor and Metonymy at the Crossroads: A Cognitive Perspective*, edited by Antonio Barcelona, 1–30. Berlin and New York: Mouton de Gruyter, 2000.

Barthes, Roland. *Camera Lucida: Reflections on Photography.* 1981. Translated by Richard Howard. New York: Hill and Wang, 2000.

———. *A Lover's Discourse: Fragments.* 1979. Translated by Richard Howard. New York: Hill and Wang, 2000.

Bauman, Richard. "Introduction." In *Folklore and Culture on the Texas-Mexican Border*, by Américo Paredes, edited by Richard Bauman, ix–xxiii. Austin: CMAS Books, 1993.

Bellah, Robert. "Civil Religion in America." In *The Robert Bellah Reader*, edited by Robert N. Bellah and Steven M. Tipton, 225–43. Durham, NC: Duke University Press, 2006.

Bercovitch, Sacvan. "Games of Chess: A Model of Literary and Cultural

Studies." In *Centuries' Ends, Narrative Means*, edited by Robert Newman, 15–57. Stanford, CA: Stanford University Press, 1996.

———. "A Model of Cultural Transvaluation: Puritanism, Modernity, and New World Rhetoric." Paper presented at Early Modern Trans-Atlantic Encounters: England, Spain and the Americas, City University of New York, March 6–7, 1997. http://web.gc.cuny.edu/dept/renai/conf/Papers/Keynote/Bercovit.htm.

Berry, Ellen N., and Mikhail N. Epstein. *Transcultural Experiments: Russian and American Models of Creative Communication*. New York: St. Martin's Press, 1999.

Beuka, Robert. *SuburbiaNation*. New York: Macmillan Palgrave, 2004.

Bhabha, Homi. "The Third Space: Interview with Homi Bhabha." In *Identity, Community, Culture, Difference*, edited by J. Rutherford, 207–21. London: Lawrence and Wishart, 1990.

Blake, David Haven, and Michael Robertson, eds. *Walt Whitman: Where the Future Becomes Present*. Iowa City: University of Iowa Press, 2008.

Boden, Anna, and Ryan Fleck. *Sugar*. Motion picture. Directed by Anna Boden and Ryan Fleck. New York: JourneyMan Pictures, 2008.

Bruce-Novoa, Juan. *Retro-Space: Collected Essays on Chicano Literature*. Houston: Arte Público Press, 1990.

Castoriadis, Cornelius. *Figures of the Thinkable*. Translated by Helen Arnold. Stanford, CA: Stanford University Press, 2007.

———. *The Imaginary Institution of Society*. Cambridge, MA: MIT Press, 1987.

Crèvecoeur, J. Hector St. John de. "Letter III. What is an American?" In *Letters from an American Farmer*, introduced by William Peterfield Trent and Ludwig Lewisohn. New York: Fox, Duffield and Company, 1904.

Dailey, Thomas. "Believing in Baseball: the Religious Power of Our National Pastime." *Logos* 6, no. 2 (2003): 63–83.

Deleuze, Gilles. *Francis Bacon: The Logic of Sensation*. Translated by Daniel W. Smith. London and New York: Continuum, 2003.

Dirlik, Arif. "American Studies in the Time of Empire." *Comparative American Studies* 2, no. 3 (2004): 287–302.

Dupuey, Edward. "The Confessions of an Ex-Suicide: Relenting and Recovering in Richard Ford's *The Sportswriter*." In Guagliardo, *Perspectives on Richard Ford*, 71–82.

Egeland, Steinar. "Festschrift." Kvinesdal: Steinar Egeland, 1992.

Emerson, Ralph Waldo. "The Poet." In *The Collected Works of Ralph Waldo Emerson, Vol. III: Essays: Second Series*, edited by Alfred R.

Ferguson and Jean Ferguson Carr, introduced by Joseph Slater, 3–24. Cambridge, MA: The Belknap Press of Harvard University Press, 1983.
———. "The Transcendentalist." In *The Collected Works of Ralph Waldo Emerson, Volume I: Nature, Addresses, and Lectures*, edited by Alfred R. Ferguson, introduced by Robert E. Spiller, 201–16. Cambridge, MA: The Belknap Press of Harvard University Press, 1971.

Fluck, Winfried. "Theories of American Culture." Paper delivered at Transatlantic American Studies: Transcultural Vision of Identities in Images and Text, Humboldt University, Berlin, February 2005.

Font, Mauricio Augusto, Alfonso W. Quiroz, and Pamela Maria Smorkanoff. "Introduction: The Intellectual Legacy of Fernando Ortiz." In *Cuban Counterpoints: The Legacy of Fernando Ortiz*, edited by Mauricio A. Font and Alfonso W. Quiroz, xi–xix. Lanham, MD: Lexington Books, 2005.

Ford, Richard. *The Sportswriter*. 1986. London: Vintage, 2003.

Foucault, Michel. "Of Other Spaces." In *Heterotopia and the City: Public Space in a Postcivil Society*, edited by Lieven de Cauter and Michiel Dehane, 14–26. London: Routledge, 2008.

Genette, Gerard. *Figures of Literary Discourse*. Translated by Alan Sheridan. Introduced by Marie-Rose Logan. New York: Columbia University Press, 1982.

Geuss, Raymond. "Kultur, Bildung, Geist." *History and Theory* 35, no. 2 (1996): 151–64.

Gilbertson, Oswald I. *Sånn va dæ då i Kvinesdal: Som æg minnest dæ . . .* [The way it was then in Kvinesdal: As I recall it . . .]. Oswald Gilbertson, 1998.

Gómez-Peña, Guillermo. *Ethno-Techno: Writings on Performance, Activism, and Pedagogy*. London: Taylor and Francis, 2005.

Gonzales, Rodolfo. *I am Joaquín*. New York: Bantam Books, 1975.

Görling, Reinhold. "Topology of Borders in Turkish-German Cinema." In *Border Poetics De-limited*, edited by Johan Schimanski and Stephen Wolfe, 149–62. Hannover: Wehrhahn Verlag, 2004.

Gruesz, Kirsten Silvia. "Walt Whitman, Latino Poet." In Blake and Robertson, *Walt Whitman*, 151–76.

Grønstad, Asbjørn, and Lene Johannessen. *To Become the Self One Is: A Critical Companion to "A Saloonkeeper's Daughter."* Oslo: Novus Press, 2005.

Guagliardo, Huey, ed. *Perspectives on Richard Ford*. Jackson: University Press of Mississippi, 2000.

Gulliksen, Øyvind. "The Lutheran Immigrant Turns Unitarian: Bjørnstjerne Bjørnson, William Ellery Channing, and Religious Idealism in *A Saloonkeeper's Daughter*." In Grønstad and Johannessen, *To Become the Self One Is*, 15–30.

Gutiérrez, David G. *Walls and Mirrors: Mexican Americans, Mexican Immigrants, and the Politics of Ethnicity*. Berkeley: University of California Press, 1995.

Hardin, James. *Reflection and Action: Essays on the Bildungsroman*. Columbia: University of South Carolina Press, 1991.

Hobson, Fred. "*The Sportswriter*: Post-Faulkner, Post-Southern?" In Guagliardo, *Perspectives on Richard Ford*, 83–96.

Holt, Hamilton. "Life Story of a Lithuanian." In *The Life Stories of Undistinguished Americans as Told by Themselves*, edited by Hamilton Holt, introduced by Werner Sollors, 6–20. New York and London: Routledge, 2000 [1906].

Horsman, Reginald. *Race and Manifest Destiny: The Origins of American Racial Anglo-Saxonism*. Cambridge, MA: Harvard University Press, 1981.

Hughes, Langston. "I, Too." In *The Collected Poems of Langston Hughes*, edited by A. Rampersad, 46. New York: Vintage, 1995.

Huntington, Samuel. *The Clash of Civilizations and the Remaking of World Order*. New York: Simon and Schuster, 1996.

———. "The Hispanic Challenge." *Foreign Policy* (March/April 2004): 30–45. http://www.foreignpolicy.com/articles/2004/03/01/the_hispanic_challenge.

———. "The Special Case of Mexican Immigration." *The American Enterprise Online* 11 (December 2000): 20–22.

———. *Who Are We? The Challenges to America's Identity*. New York: Simon and Schuster, 2004.

Huyssen, Andreas. "Present Pasts: Media , Politics, Amnesia." In *Globalization*, edited by Arjun Appadurai, 57–77. Durham, NC: Duke University Press, 2001.

Jacobson, Roman. "Two Aspects of Language and Two Types of Aphasic Disturbances." In *Fundamentals of Language*, edited by Roman Jacobson and Morris Halle, 49–70. The Hague: Mouton, 1971.

Janson, Drude Krog. *A Saloonkeeper's Daughter*. Edited with an introduction by Orm Øverland. Translated by Gerald Thorson. Baltimore: Johns Hopkins University Press, 2002.

Kadir, Djelal. "Introduction: America and Its Studies." *PMLA* 118, no. 1 (2003): 9–24.

Klahn, Norma. "Chicana and Mexicana Feminist Practices: De/Linking Cultural Imaginaries." In *Genealogies of Displacement: Diaspora/Exile/Migration and Chicana/o/Latina/o/Latin American/Peninsular Literary and Cultural Studies*, edited by Jordi Aladro, Norma Klahn, Lourdes Martínez-Echazábal, and Juan Poblete, 163–74. *Nuevo Texto Critico* 29/32, 2002–03.

Knox, Paul. "Vulgaria: The Re-Enchantment of Suburbia." *Opolis: An International Journal of Suburban and Metropolitan Studies* 1, no. 2 (2005): 33–46.

Koselleck, Richard. *The Practice of Conceptual History: Timing History, Spacing Concepts*. Stanford, CA: Stanford University Press, 2002.

Lacan, Jacques. *Ecrits: A Selection*. Edited by Bruce Fink and Heloise Fink. Translated by Russell Grigg. New York: W. W. Norton and Company, 2004.

Lazare, Daniel. "Diversity and Its Discontents." *The Nation*, May 27, 2004, 1–5. http://www.thenation.com/article/diversity-and-its-discontents.

Limón, José E. *Mexican Ballads, Chicano Poems: History and Influence in Mexican-American Social Poetry*. Berkeley: University of California Press, 1992.

Lodge, David. *The Modes of Modern Writing: Metaphor, Metonymy, and the Typology of Modern Literature*. London: Hodder Arnold, 1977.

Lowenthal, David. *The Past Is a Foreign Country*. Cambridge: Cambridge University Press, 1990.

Luebbering, Ken. "Redefining 'American': The Creation of Identity in *A Saloonkeeper's Daughter*." In Grønstad and Johannessen, *To Become the Self One Is*, 57–66.

Madsen, Deborah. "Keynote Lecture." The Salzburg Global Seminar, Transnationalism and Immigration Shock in American Society and Literature, Salzburg, Austria, October 30–November 2, 2008.

Massey, Doreen B. *For Space*. London: Sage Publications, 2005.

Massey, Doreen B. *Space, Place, and Gender*. Cambridge: Polity Press, 1994.

McClennen, Sophia A. "Inter-American Studies or Imperial American Studies?" *Comparative American Studies* 3, no. 4 (2005): 393–413.

Meier, Matt, and Feliciano Ribera. *Mexican Americans/American Mexicans: From Conquistadors to Chicanos*. New York: Hill and Wang, 1995.

Menand, Louis. "Patriot Games: The New Nativism of Samuel P. Huntington." *The New Yorker*, May 17, 2004. http://www.newyorker.com/archive/2004/05/17/040517crbo_books.

Menéndez, Ana. *In Cuba I Was a German Shepherd*. New York: Grove Press, 2001.

Mignolo, Walter D., and Freya Schiwy. "Beyond Dichotomies: Translation/Transculturation and the Colonial Difference." In *Beyond Dichotomies: Histories, Identities, Cultures, and the Challenge of Globalization*, edited by Elisabeth Mudimbe-Boyi, 251–86. New York: SUNY Press, 2002.

Moretti, Franco. *The Way of the World: The Bildungsroman in European Culture*. London: Verso, 1987.

Mumford, Lewis. *The City in History: Its Origins, Its Transformations, and Its Prospects*. New York: Harcourt, Brace and World, 1961.

Nabokov, Vladimir. *Pnin*. London: Heinemann, 1957.

Nicholson, Philip Y. "The Elusive Soul of the Suburbs: An Inquiry into Contemporary Political Culture." In *Suburbia Re-examined*, edited by Barbara M. Kelly, 207–14. New York: Greenwood Press, 1989.

Nissen, Axel. "*A Saloonkeeper's Daughter* in the Company of Women." In Grønstad and Johannessen, *To Become the Self One Is*, 115–30.

O'Hehir, Andrew. "Sugar: Best Baseball Movie Ever." *Salon*, April 3, 2009. http://www.salon.com/ent/movies/btm/feature/2009/04/03/sugar/index.html.

Owens, Bill. *Suburbia*. San Francisco: Straight Arrow Books, 1972.

Paredes, Américo. *"With His Pistol in His Hand": A Border Ballad and Its Hero*. Austin: University of Texas Press, 1990.

Ringdal, Siv. *Det Amerikanske Lista: Med 110 Volt i Huset*. Oslo: Pax, 2002.

Rodriguez, Richard. *Brown: The Last Discovery of America*. New York: Viking, 2002.

———. *Days of Obligation: An Argument with My Mexican Father*. New York: Viking, 1992.

———. Interview in Lene Johannessen, "Amerikas Historier på Langs." [America's stories: Perpendicular], *Replikk* 26 (2008): 16–23.

Rønning, Anne Holden. "*A Saloonkeeper's Daughter* and the Woman Question." In Grønstad and Johannessen, *To Become the Self One Is*, 31–42.

Said, Edward. "The Clash of Ignorance." *The Nation*, October 22, 2001. http://www.thenation.com/article/clash-ignorance.

Saldívar, Ramón. *Chicano Narrative: The Dialectics of Difference*. Madison: University of Wisconsin Press, 1990.

Sammons, Jeffrey. "The Bildungsroman for Nonspecialists: An Attempt at a Clarification." In Hardin, *Reflection and Action*, 26–45.

Seidel, Michael. *Exile and the Narrative Imagination*. New Haven, CT: Yale University Press, 1986.

Sokel, Walter. "The Blackening of the Breast: The Narrative of Existential Education and R. M. Rilke's *The Notebooks of Malte Brigge*." In Hardin, *Reflection and Action*, 329–61.

The State Museum of Pennsylvania. "Becoming a Levittowner: Community Life," *Saturday Evening Post*, 1954. In "Levittown, Pa.: Building the Suburban Dream," 2003. http://web1.fandm.edu/levittown/default.html.

Taylor, Charles. "Buffered and Porous Selves." Comment on *The Secular Age*. At *The Immanent Frame*, edited by Jonathan Van Antwerpen. Social Science Research Council Blog. http://www.ssrc.org/blogs/immanent_frame/.

Taylor, Charles. *Modern Social Imaginaries*. Durham, NC: Duke University Press, 2002.

Thompson, Dianne Oenning. *The Brothers Karamazov and the Poetics of Memory*. Cambridge: Cambridge University Press, 1991.

Thorson, Gerald. Translator's preface to Janson, *A Saloonkeeper's Daughter*, ix–x.

Ugarte, Michael. *Shifting Ground: Spanish Civil War Exile Literature*. Durham, NC: Duke University Press, 1989.

White, Hayden. "Good of Their Kind." *New Literary History* 34 (2003): 367–76.

———. *Metahistory: The Historical Imagination in Nineteenth-Century Europe*. Baltimore: Johns Hopkins University Press, 1975.

———. *Tropics of Discourse: Essays in Cultural Criticism*. Baltimore: Johns Hopkins University Press, 1978.

Whitman, Walt. "Song of Myself." In *Leaves of Grass* ("Death-Bed Edition.") Introduction by William Carlos Williams. New York: The Modern Library, 2000.

Wilcox, Phyllis Perrin. *Metaphor in American Sign Language*. Washington, D.C.: Gallaudet University Press, 2000.

Wolfe, Alan. "Native Son: Samuel Huntington Defends the Homeland." *Foreign Affairs* May/June, 2004.

Zirin, Dave. "Say It Ain't So, Big Leagues." *The Nation*, October 26, 2005. http://www.thenation.com/article/say-it-aint-so-big-leagues?page=0,0.

Øverland, Orm. *Immigrant Minds, American Identities: Making the United States Home, 1870–1930*. Urbana and Chicago: University of Illinois Press, 2000.

Øverland, Orm. Introduction to Janson, *A Saloonkeeper's Daughter*, xi–xxxiv.

Årli, Ånen. *Kvinesdal: Ei Bygdebok*, Vol. 3. Flekkefjord: Hegland Boktrykkeri, 1972.

INDEX